# Texas Assessment Preparation

Grade 6

HOLT McDOUGAL

## Literature

Texas

### TEXAS WRITE SOURCE

 HOUGHTON MIFFLIN HARCOURT

# Contents

© Houghton Mifflin Harcourt Publishing Company

## Written Composition

## Revising and Editing

## PART II: *TEXAS WRITE SOURCE* ASSESSMENTS

Contents

# How to Use This Book

*Texas Assessment Preparation* contains instruction that will help you develop the reading and writing skills tested on the State of Texas Assessments of Academic Readiness (STAAR). In addition, this book includes tests that accompany the Houghton Mifflin Harcourt *Texas Write Source* program.

## PART I: PREPARING FOR TEXAS ASSESSMENTS

Part I of the book will help you develop skills assessed on the STAAR test. It consists of two basic types of instruction:

- **Guided instruction** materials offer annotations, citations from the Texas Essential Knowledge and Skills (TEKS), and answer explanations, plus models and rubrics for written composition. Annotations highlight the key skills you will need to apply. Sample questions, answer explanations, models, and rubrics help you analyze each question or prompt and its correct response.

- **Practice** materials give you the opportunity to apply what you have learned to assessments like those you will be taking near the end of your school year.

Part I is divided into the following sections:

## Reading

The readings from a variety of genres give you opportunities to practice the essential reading skills outlined in the TEKS for your grade. Initially, as you read the Guided Reading passages, annotations and shading offer detailed explanations that draw attention to specific TEKS-based skills. After you have finished reading, you can review and hone test-taking skills by analyzing sample multiple-choice items, their answers, and answer explanations. Following guided instruction, you will independently practice essential reading and assessment skills. For these Reading Practice lessons, you will read selections and answer multiple-choice items crafted to cover a range of appropriate TEKS and reading comprehension skills.

One feature of the Reading Practice materials in this book is a column headed "**My notes about what I am reading.**" You can improve your comprehension skills by using this column to monitor your reading abilities.

As you read the Reading Practice selections, take advantage of the "My notes about what I am reading" column by using it to make notes about the following topics:

- Key ideas or events

- Initial or overall impressions of characters, situations, or topics, including how each is like someone or something familiar to you

- Guesses at the meaning of any unfamiliar words or phrases

- Questions or points of confusion

- Ideas about why the author wrote the selection

- Comments about what you would like to know more about

- Your own ideas about the meaning of ideas or events or how they might apply to the real world

In addition, you may want to mark the selection text itself. You can, for example, circle, underscore, or highlight words or phrases that seem important or about which you have questions.

## Written Composition

This section provides you with model essay prompts, sample essays, and scoring rubrics. These resources give you opportunities to practice the writing process for genres that will be tested. First, annotations will guide you as you analyze sample prompts and 2- and 4-point model responses. Then, you will practice your writing skills independently by responding to similar TEKS-aligned prompts.

## Revising and Editing

In the multiple-choice format of this section, you will practice TEKS-based revising and editing skills. First, you will receive guided instruction in revising or editing. You will read sample essays, review assessment items, and analyze answer explanations. Then, you will work on independent practice, in which you identify editing or revising issues in sample essays and answer multiple-choice items crafted to cover a range of appropriate revising or editing TEKS.

## PART II: *TEXAS WRITE SOURCE* ASSESSMENTS

The *Texas Write Source* assessments are a set of four tests designed to help you measure your progress in *Texas Write Source*.

- The **Pretest** should be completed at the beginning of the school year. It can help you measure your level of writing experience and knowledge and what your teacher might need to emphasize in your instruction. The **Pretest** also provides a baseline for measuring your progress from the beginning of the year to the end.

- **Progress Test 1** and **Progress Test 2** should be completed at regular intervals during the year. These tests can help you and your teacher monitor your progress as the school year proceeds.

- The **Post-test** should be completed at the end of the year to show how much progress you have made.

Each test has three parts. *Part 1: Basic Elements of Writing* and *Part 2: Proofreading and Editing* comprise a total of 30 multiple-choice questions. You will choose the best answer to each question. *Part 3: Writing* provides a writing prompt. You will respond by writing a composition.

---

NOTE: Every effort has been made to incorporate the latest information available about STAAR at the time of publication.

---

# Part I

# Preparing for Texas Assessments

# Guided Reading

# Reading Literary Text: Fiction

In this part of the book, you will read a short story with instruction about the elements of fiction. Following the selection are sample questions and answers about the story. The purpose of this section is to show you how to understand and analyze fiction.

To begin, review the TEKS that relate to fiction:

| FICTION TEKS | WHAT IT MEANS TO YOU |
|---|---|
| **(6) Comprehension of Literary Text/Fiction** Students understand, make inferences and draw conclusions about the structure and elements of fiction and provide evidence from text to support their understanding. Students are expected to: | |
| (A) summarize the elements of plot development (e.g., rising action, turning point, climax, falling action, denouement) in various works of fiction; | You will explain the different parts of a plot, including rising action, turning point, climax, falling action, and denouement, in a story. |
| (B) recognize dialect and conversational voice and explain how authors use dialect to convey character; and | You will recognize dialect (language spoken in a particular area or by a particular group) and discuss how authors portray their characters through speech. |
| (C) describe different forms of point-of-view, including first- and third-person. | You will understand the different points of view from which a story is told, including first-person and third-person point of view. |

The selection that follows provides instruction on the fiction TEKS as well as other TEKS. It also covers reading comprehension skills, such as making inferences about text.

As you read the story "Danny's Surprise," notice how the author builds the action toward an exciting climax. The annotations in the margins will guide you as you read.

# Guided Reading

| Read this selection. Then answer the questions that follow. |
| --- |

## Danny's Surprise

1   Danny dragged the heavy, green trash bag out the front door. "There must be a ton of bricks in this thing," he thought to himself. Slowly, he heaved it, step by step, toward the bin at the corner of the house, pausing to wipe the stinging sweat out of his eyes. For the past week, the temperature had been over a hundred degrees, making the air outside feel like the inside of a blast furnace. With any luck, it would be a little cooler by that evening. His mom, his sister, and he were going to the park to watch the Fourth of July fireworks, accompanied by Danny's two best friends, Sonya and Rafael.

2   Danny, Sonya, and Rafael liked to spend time together whenever they could. An only child, Sonya said hanging out with Danny and Rafael was like having two brothers. Rafael, the youngest of five kids, said he enjoyed being with people his own age "for a change." For Danny, having fun with Sonya and Rafael was a break from helping out at home.

3   The three of them had started playing jokes on each other early in the summer—never anything dangerous or harmful, just a prank that ended with flour all over someone's face or a mouthful of mouthwash instead of lemonade. Rafael had started it. He claimed he was tired of always being the target of his brothers' and sisters' jokes.

4   "Besides," he said, "Sonya needs to know what having brothers is really like."

5   As Danny wrestled the trash bag around the corner of the house, he suddenly stopped. He had heard something. "Ssh! Sonya, keep it down! We don't want Danny to find out our plans." Rafael's voice came from the bushes near the trash bin.

### POINT OF VIEW
In literature, a narrator tells the story. The author's choice of narrator is referred to as point of view. The first two sentences in paragraph 1 contain clues to the point of view in this story. Because the narrator is outside the story and describes the thoughts and feelings of only one character (Danny), the point of view is third-person limited.

**TEKS 6C; Fig. 19D**

### MAKING INFERENCES
As you read fiction, you often need to make inferences, or draw conclusions based on details in the text and your own knowledge and experience. For example, you can infer from Rafael's conversation with Sonya in paragraph 5 that the two of them are planning a prank on Danny.

**Fig. 19D**

GO ON

6     Danny set the trash bag down and noiselessly sprinted to the front door. He was careful not to let the screen door bang behind him. He dashed through the house, burst out the back door, and crept up to the low brick wall that separated the front yard from the back. He was in a great position to eavesdrop on the two plotters.

7     "When he comes outside to look for us," Rafael was saying, "you hit the button to turn on the sprinklers."

8     "But how will we get him to stand in the right place?" Sonya wanted to know.

9     "I'm gonna hide behind the elm tree and . . . listen." Rafael twisted his mouth and produced a whine like a tiny puppy. Sonya snorted with laughter.

10     "That's perfect!" she said. "You know how much Danny wants a dog! I reckon he'll go right after it." After listening to the rest of his friends' conversation, Danny sneaked from his hiding place. Thinking furiously, he made a few plans of his own.

11     Rafael and Sonya arrived late that evening. As his mother gathered up sandwiches and cold drinks to take to the park, Danny went outside, pretending to look for his friends. Sure enough, he heard the faint cry of a puppy.

12     Trying not to grin, he paced around the bushes at the front of the house, tracking down the sound. He avoided the sprinkler controls at the side, where he knew Sonya crouched. The puppy's whining seemed to be coming from the elm tree by the sidewalk. Danny headed in that direction.

13     "Hey, y'all, where are you?" he called to Rafael and Sonya. "I've found a puppy. At least, I can hear one. Nice fella," he murmured, peering into the dusk. As he approached the tree, from the corner of his eye he saw Sonya's hand moving toward the sprinkler controls. A second later the sprinklers erupted in a blast of cold water.

> **DIALECT**
> Dialect is the form of a language that is spoken by a particular group of people—often the people who live in a specific region. Authors often use dialect to help make a character realistic. In paragraph 10, "I reckon" is an example of dialect.
>
> **TEKS 6B**

14    Rafael yelled and jumped from behind the tree. Sonya screamed, bringing Danny's mother to the door. Meanwhile, Danny's sides were splitting as he watched their antics. Rafael raced from the sprinkler, which Danny had secretly turned toward the tree, and Sonya scrambled out of the bushes. By the time Mrs. Hernandez shut off the sprinklers, both were soaked, their dripping hair hanging in strings, their t-shirts and shorts sagging from the weight of the water in them. As Danny continued to howl, Sonya and Rafael stood gasping, shocked by this unexpected ending to their scheme. In a moment, though, they too were laughing, doubled over as water dripped from them.

15    "Nice job watering the lawn, you guys," Mrs. Hernandez said, with an amused smile on her face. "Now, if you two want to get dried off, we have some fireworks to go see."

**PLOT DEVELOPMENT**
Paragraph 14 describes the climax of the story, when the conflict reaches its most intense and exciting moment. In this part of the story, we learn how the conflict between Danny and his friends is resolved.

**TEKS 6A**

GO ON

---

**Use "Danny's Surprise" (pp. 5–7) to answer questions 1–4.**

---

1 One example of dialect in this story is —

A *"You know how much Danny wants a dog!"*

B *"That's perfect!"*

C *"Hey, y'all, where are you?"*

D *"At least, I can hear one."*

> **EXPLANATION:** The word *y'all* is an example of dialect; it is a contraction of the words *you* and *all* used by Southern speakers of English. **C** is correct. **A, B,** and **D** are incorrect; these standard English words and phrases are used by English speakers everywhere.

**TEKS 6B**

2 A story usually has a main conflict, or problem, that the characters need to resolve. In the rising action, events happen as a result of the conflict. The rising action ends with the story's climax. Which of the following takes place during the rising action of "Danny's Surprise"?

F Danny drags a heavy bag of trash out of his house.

G Sonya, Rafael, and Danny plan to watch the Fourth of July fireworks.

H Danny hears a sound like a puppy and walks toward it.

J Mrs. Hernandez suggests that Sonya and Rafael dry off.

> **EXPLANATION:** The conflict in this story is between Danny and his friends. Sonya and Rafael plan to play a prank on Danny, but Danny wants to outsmart them. As a result, he pretends to go along with their prank when Rafael makes a sound like a puppy. **H** is correct.
> - **F** is incorrect. Danny puts out the trash at the very beginning of the story, before the conflict is introduced.
> - **G** is incorrect. The characters make their plan to watch the fireworks before the story begins.
> - **J** is incorrect. This event occurs after Danny has played his trick on Sonya and Rafael, which resolves the conflict.

**TEKS 6A; Fig. 19D, 19E**

**3** The point of view in this story helps you understand —

**A** why Rafael and Sonya's plan backfires

**B** how Danny's mother feels about the three friends' nonstop pranks

**C** what Rafael is thinking when he gets wet

**D** how Sonya plans to get back at Danny

> **EXPLANATION:** The third-person narrator in this story tells readers only Danny's thoughts and feelings. In paragraph 10, after Danny hears Sonya and Rafael's plans, the narrator says that Danny "made a few plans of his own." In other words, he changes the sprinklers to trick his friends. **A** is correct.
> - **B** and **C** are incorrect. The narrator is limited to describing Danny's thoughts and feelings. The story doesn't tell what Danny's mother and Rafael think or feel.
> - **D** is incorrect. The story does not tell how Sonya plans to get back at Danny.

**TEKS 6C; Fig. 19D**

**4** In the climax of this story, the reader learns that —

**F** Rafael and Sonya plan to trick Danny

**G** Rafael and Sonya got Danny a dog

**H** the three friends like to play tricks

**J** Danny has tricked Rafael and Sonya

> **EXPLANATION:** The climax (paragraph 14) reveals that Danny has tricked his friends by rearranging the sprinklers so they will get soaked instead of him. **J** is correct.
> - **F** is incorrect because Rafael and Sonya's plan is revealed before the climax.
> - **G** is incorrect. The friends plan to use the sound of a puppy to lure Danny out onto the lawn, but they do not get Danny a real dog.
> - **H** is incorrect. This information is presented before the climax.

**TEKS 6A**

STOP

# Reading Literary Text: Literary Nonfiction

In this part of the book, you will read a personal narrative with instruction about the elements of literary nonfiction. Following the selection are sample questions and answers about the personal narrative. The purpose of this section is to show you how to understand and analyze literary nonfiction.

To begin, review the TEKS that relate to literary nonfiction:

| LITERARY NONFICTION TEKS | WHAT IT MEANS TO YOU |
|---|---|
| **(7) Comprehension of Literary Text/Literary Nonfiction** Students understand, make inferences and draw conclusions about the varied structural patterns and features of literary nonfiction and provide evidence from text to support their understanding. Students are expected to identify the literary language and devices used in memoirs and personal narratives and compare their characteristics with those of an autobiography. | You will understand and draw conclusions about the way nonfiction is put together and support your analysis with examples from the text. You will also recognize how the language and devices used in memoirs and personal stories are different from those used in autobiographies. |

The selection that follows provides instruction on the literary nonfiction TEKS as well as other TEKS. It also covers reading comprehension skills, such as making inferences and synthesizing text to understand its structure.

As you read the personal narrative "Rock Climbing: Man and Mountain," notice how the author organizes and describes his ideas. The annotations in the margins will guide you as you read.

# Guided Reading

| |
| --- |
| **Read this selection. Then answer the questions that follow.** |

## Rock Climbing: Man and Mountain

1    When I rock climb, I'm free. To me, rock climbing isn't just exercise; it's an art and a spiritual journey. I climb because I find satisfaction in the movement—it's a dance, and the mountain is my partner. Each time I climb, I have the challenge of adjusting my moves to find the rhythm and style that will fit my partner. Each mountain is also a goal. I visualize myself reaching the summit. I prepare mentally, physically, and emotionally. When I succeed, I feel a tremendous strength and a sense of accomplishment. My mountain climbing successes have taught me that I can approach my life's goals in the same way.

2    Climbing has also taught me that there is a difference between good fears and bad fears. Good fears keep you safe and make you double-check what you are doing, while bad fears stop you from doing something that really is safe.

3    My name is Joe, and I started rock climbing when I found out that I could do it. I'd walked by the "rock climbing wall" at my gym dozens of times before I even considered trying to climb. Then, one day I heard an instructor say that anyone who can walk up a few flights of stairs without having to rest could rock climb. I was worried that I didn't have enough upper body strength. After my first lesson, though, I learned that my legs would push me up the rocks, and my arms just balanced me.

4    Now, my friend Jim and I are fanatic climbers. Last Friday night we drove up to the Catskill Mountains for a Saturday morning hike. We started out just before 5:30. I thought we were making good time up the four-mile trail. We followed a creek with water so clear that it looked like a ribbon of glass, shattering every so often on the sharp rocks in the bed. The gurgling and babbling sounds of the water calmed me. They chanted, "breathe in, breathe out, breathe in, breathe out." Before long, the sun was rising in the sky.

**ELEMENTS OF LITERARY NONFICTION**
This selection is a personal narrative. In this kind of writing, the author shares some personal experiences and tells why they were meaningful. In paragraph 1, the author uses the words "art" and "a spiritual journey" to describe rock climbing. He also compares rock climbing to a dance. These descriptions reflect a very personal view of rock climbing. In paragraph 2, the author shares some lessons he has learned from rock climbing.

**TEKS 7**

**CONTEXT CLUES**
If you don't know the word *fanatic* in paragraph 4, look for context clues. Because the author and his friend drive a distance to start a hike at 5:30 in the morning, you can guess that *fanatic* means "eager" or "very enthusiastic."

**TEKS 2B**

GO ON ➤

5    We were close to reaching the rock face, the "wall" we were going to climb. I was surprised by the steady incline we had to ascend to get to the real climbing spot. We'd already broken a good sweat. Usually, we don't have to work so hard before "really" climbing. I was relieved that some other climbers had left their ropes. Jim and I used them, even though they did not lead straight up to our route. We zigzagged up until we came to a level spot. Jim stumbled up behind me, and when I asked him how he was feeling, he answered by throwing up on my boots. I suggested that we remove our backpacks and sit down and rest for a while. Jim agreed.

6    We took a break. Through the silence that wrapped around us, we could hear the birds chattering and the wind whistling a gentle tune. After a few minutes, I told Jim that I understood if he wanted to quit. But being a determined fellow, he shook his head *no* and slung his backpack over his shoulders.

**FIGURATIVE LANGUAGE**
In paragraph 6, the author describes the setting of his climb using personification, giving human characteristics to the birds and the wind.

**TEKS 8**

7    From the level ground, we scrambled up a dirt crevice until we reached the base of our climb. The gap was dirty and slick. I checked my watch; we had about nine hours of daylight left. I was annoyed that we'd wasted all that time just getting to this spot, so I quickly scaled the first pitch. A pitch is about fifteen feet of climbing. This pitch wasn't too steep, so I didn't bother to put any gear in the rock to help me. I looked over my shoulder for Jim, and, although he looked ghostly, he shimmied up the pitch. Soon we were at the base of the chimney, a wide crack in the rock big enough to fit most of your body.

**CONTEXT CLUES**
When you come across technical terms that you do not recognize, read further. The author may include a definition or an explanation later in the text. In paragraph 7, the author defines the climbing terms *pitch* and *chimney* soon after their first use.

**TEKS 2B**

8    As I climbed the chimney, the jagged edges and harsh sandpaper surface scraped my arms and legs. I was glad I was wearing kneepads. Getting out of the chimney and onto the next ledge was tough, so I fixed a rope to a tree and heaved myself up. Panting, I leaned over to catch my breath and wipe the sweat out of my eyes while Jim made his way to the top.

9    The next pitch was steep—in fact, completely vertical—so I pulled out my climbing aids. We were going to have to belay, or assist each other. I secured my ropes through a harness and tied myself in it. I was the lead climber, so I went first. Once I reached the ledge, I helped Jim up the slope.

10    We climbed the next section with protection—solid cams. Camming devices—also called cams or friends—are used mainly to protect the lead climber from falling. A cam has a trigger that allows it to widen to fit into different-sized cracks. I use cams so I can shift my weight onto them while I climb up a steep slope. I moved very slowly to make sure that the cams didn't pull out, and, finally, I made it to the top.

11    When Jim caught up with me, we prepared our camp. First, we made sure that everything, including ourselves, was carefully clipped and secured so nothing would roll away at night. Since I'm bigger than Jim, I decided to sleep on a flat boulder while Jim squeezed in a slot between my boulder and the wall face. Then I allowed myself to feel exhausted.

12    I'd gone for so long without food or water that I was dizzy, but after I forced myself to eat and drink, I revived enough to soak in the warmth of the evening. The stars directly above our heads glinted like gold confetti sprinkled across the dark sky, reminding me of how far we had come and how far we had left to go. Then I slept—even though the boulder was not a comfortable bed.

13    Waking at dawn, Jim and I both felt worn out, but we knew that we had to get climbing if we were going to have any chance of reaching the mountaintop.

**ELEMENTS OF LITERARY NONFICTION**
In paragraphs 7–9, concrete details, sensory language (words and phrases that appeal to the five senses), and the use of specific climbing terms convey the difficulty of the climb.

**TEKS 7, 8**

**MAKING INFERENCES**
When you infer, you combine ideas in the text with your own prior knowledge to draw a conclusion. The author's actions in paragraph 11 tell you that he is cautious and thorough.

**Fig. 19D**

**ELEMENTS OF LITERARY NONFICTION**
This last paragraph conveys a message that can be applied to life as well as to rock climbing.

**TEKS 7**

GO ON

---

**Use "Rock Climbing: Man and Mountain" (pp. 11–13) to answer questions 1–7.**

---

**1** With which idea about rock climbing would the author most likely agree?

  **A** It can be seen as a metaphor for life.

  **B** It is a dangerous sport for experts only.

  **C** It is a very expensive sport.

  **D** It is simply a fun way to pass the time.

**EXPLANATION:** The author thinks of rock climbing as more than a sport. He has learned lessons from it that he has applied to his life. He clearly sees connections between the activity and life itself, so **A** is correct.

- **B** is incorrect. In paragraph 3, the author makes the point that anyone who can climb up stairs can climb rocks.
- **C** is incorrect. Although mountain climbing might be an expensive sport, the author never mentions this. Therefore, you can make no inference about his view.
- **D** is incorrect. In paragraph 1, the author says that rock climbing is more than just exercise; "it's an art and a spiritual journey."

**TEKS 7; Fig. 19D**

**2** Which of the following is an example of a simile?

  **F** *he looked ghostly*

  **G** *I revived enough to soak in the warmth of the evening*

  **H** *the stars directly above our heads glinted like gold confetti*

  **J** *each mountain is also a goal*

**EXPLANATION:** A simile is a comparison between two unlike objects using the word *like* or *as*. **H** is correct. The stars are compared to gold confetti.

- **F** and **J** are incorrect. Both involve comparisons, but neither uses *like* or *as*.
- **G** is incorrect. This example is not a comparison.

**TEKS 7, 8**

---

GO ON ▶

**3** The author uses figurative language in paragraph 4 mainly to —

**A** show readers the obstacles climbers must overcome

**B** identify the exact geographical location of the mountain

**C** stress how important the first part of a climb is

**D** show the author's feeling of closeness to nature

> **EXPLANATION:** In paragraph 4, the author uses similes, metaphors, sensory language, and personification to describe the setting as he and his partner make their way up the incline to the mountain base. His focus on the sights and sounds of nature shows his awareness and appreciation of them. **D** is correct.
> - **A** is incorrect. There are no obstacles on the way to the base of the mountain, although the trail is surprisingly steep.
> - **B** is incorrect. The figurative language does not give any specific details of location.
> - **C** is incorrect. The language describes the surrounding nature, not the actual physical activity of the author and his partner.

**TEKS 7, 8**

**4** Which word or phrase from paragraph 7 helps you figure out the meaning of crevice?

**F** *gap*

**G** *base*

**H** *gear*

**J** *level ground*

> **EXPLANATION:** A crevice is a crack or gap in a rock or mountain. **F** is correct. **G, H,** and **J** are incorrect because they are not related to the definition of *crevice*.

**TEKS 2B**

**5** Which statement expresses the theme of this personal narrative?

**A** Some goals are too difficult to accomplish.

**B** It's important to have a hobby that you can do all by yourself.

**C** Those things that are hardest to do may be the most rewarding.

**D** Sometimes you have to stop and appreciate what you have.

> **EXPLANATION:** The theme of a work is a message about life or human nature. The author shows us that rock climbing can be difficult, that it is rewarding, and that it is necessary to keep going even when you don't feel like it. **C** is correct because it expresses the major theme of the narrative.
> - **A** is incorrect. The author does not give up when the climb gets hard; neither does his partner.
> - **B** is incorrect. The author takes a partner with him when rock climbing.
> - **D** is incorrect. This message is not supported by details throughout the narrative.

**TEKS 7**

GO ON

**6** When does a climber need to belay?

   **F** When ascending an easy slope

   **G** When attempting a difficult part of the climb

   **H** When securing the camp for the night

   **J** When approaching the wall

> **EXPLANATION:** In paragraph 9, the author tells us that to belay means to assist each other on a climb. This is necessary when a pitch is steep or there is some other difficulty connected with the climb. **G** is correct. **F, H,** and **J** are incorrect because none of these situations requires assistance.

**Fig. 19B, 19D**

**7** How would you describe the organizational structure of this narrative?

   **A** The details are narrated in strict chronological order, from the beginning to the end.

   **B** Individual topics related to rock climbing are discussed one at a time.

   **C** The least important facts about rock climbing are explained first, followed by the more important facts.

   **D** It begins with some personal thoughts followed by a true story about a particular climb.

> **EXPLANATION:** The narrative opens with the author's thoughts on rock climbing and the lessons he has learned from it. This is followed by an account of his climb, which is told in chronological order. **D** is correct.
> - **A** is incorrect. The first part of the narrative is not ordered chronologically.
> - **B** and **C** are incorrect. Information about rock climbing is given, but it is woven into the story about the climb.

**TEKS 7; Fig. 19E**

STOP

# Reading Literary Text: Poetry

In this part of the book, you will read a brief poem with instruction about the elements of poetry. Following the selection are sample questions and answers about the poem. The purpose of this section is to show you how to understand and analyze poetry.

To begin, review the TEKS that relate to poetry:

| POETRY TEKS | WHAT IT MEANS TO YOU |
|---|---|
| **(4) Comprehension of Literary Text/Poetry** Students understand, make inferences and draw conclusions about the structure and elements of poetry and provide evidence from text to support their understanding. Students are expected to explain how figurative language (e.g., personification, metaphors, similes, hyperbole) contributes to the meaning of a poem. | You will understand and draw conclusions about the way poems are put together and use examples from the poem to explain your analysis. You will also explain how figurative language, such as personification, metaphors, similes, and hyperbole, affects the meaning of the poem. |

The selection that follows provides instruction on the poetry TEKS as well as other TEKS. It also covers reading comprehension skills, such as making inferences and asking interpretive questions about text.

As you read the poem "Windy Nights," notice how the poet uses figurative language to paint a vivid picture of the wind. The annotations in the margin will guide you as you read.

# Guided Reading

Read this selection. Then answer the questions that follow.

## Windy Nights
*by Rodney Bennett*

*This poem follows the wind's evening path through the land and then back to the sea.*

Rumbling in the chimneys,
    Rattling at the doors,
Round the roofs and round the roads
    The rude wind roars;
5 Raging through the darkness,
    Raving[1] through the trees,
Racing off again across
    The great grey seas.

**ELEMENTS OF POETRY**
The poet makes generous use of alliteration, the repetition of sounds at the beginning of words. The poet also uses onomatopoeia, the use of words whose sounds echo their meanings. As you read, think about the poet's purpose in using these literary devices.

**TEKS 4**

**PERSONIFICATION**
Personification is a figure of speech in which human qualities are given to an animal, an object, or an idea. Consider the human qualities the poet gives to the wind and how this affects the poem's meaning.

**TEKS 4, 8; Fig. 19D**

1. **raving:** roaring; raging.

GO ON

**Use "Windy Nights" (p. 18) to answer questions 1–4.**

**1** The poet's use of alliteration highlights the wind's —

**A** sound and motion
**B** damp chilliness
**C** destructiveness
**D** unevenness

**EXPLANATION:** The poet repeats the *r* sound in the words *rumbling, rattling, round, roofs, roads, rude, roars, raging, raving,* and *racing.* **A** is correct. Each phrase using these words describes the action and noise of the wind.
- **B** is incorrect because the details in the poem do not tell whether the wind is warm or cold, damp or dry.
- **C** is incorrect because the wind does not cause any destruction in the poem.
- **D** is incorrect because the wind is described as a continuous force, not an uneven one.

**TEKS 4; Fig. 19B**

**2** Onomatopoeia is the use of words whose sounds echo their meanings. Which words from the poem are an example of onomatopoeia?

**F** *roofs, roads, rude*
**G** *rumbling, rattling, roars*
**H** *chimneys, trees, seas*
**J** *doors, roads, trees*

**EXPLANATION:** The words *rumbling, rattling,* and *roars* all sound like the noises they name. **G** is correct.
- **F** is incorrect. These words create the sound device of alliteration because they all begin with the letter *r,* but they are not related to the actual sounds of the wind.
- **H** is incorrect. These words rhyme, which is another kind of sound device used in poetry, but the words do not sound like what they mean.
- **J** is incorrect because none of these words is directly related to a noise or sound that the wind makes.

**TEKS 4**

**GO ON**

Name _____ Date _____

**3** The poet uses personification in lines 4 and 7 to —

A emphasize the strength and power of the wind

B express the idea that the wind is careless

C create an image of the wind as dangerous and frightening

D show that the wind is thoughtful and caring

> **EXPLANATION:** In line 4, the poet uses the adjective *rude* to describe the wind. In line 7, he describes the wind as *racing off.* Both of these human traits suggest carelessness. **B** is correct.
> • **A** is incorrect. The poem stresses the power of the wind, but not through the use of personification.
> • **C** is incorrect. The wind may seem scary and dangerous, but the poet does not use personification to create this impression.
> • **D** is incorrect. The wind is described as rude, not thoughtful and caring.

**TEKS 4, 8; Fig. 19D**

**4** Which of the following best expresses the theme, or message, of this poem?

F The wind is a powerful force of nature that cannot be controlled.

G You never know what to expect from the wind.

H People should harness the power of the wind more effectively.

J The wind can make a dark night seem even drearier.

> **EXPLANATION:** The wind rumbles, rattles, and rages on its path without regard for anything in its way. **F** is correct because all evidence in the poem supports the message that the wind is a wild, uncontrolled force.
> • **G** is incorrect. While the wind may be unpredictable, the speaker of the poem doesn't express surprise over it.
> • **H** is incorrect. Details in the poem do not relate to harnessing the wind's power.
> • **J** is incorrect because the poem focuses on the power of the wind and not how it makes people feel.

**TEKS 3A, 4; Fig. 19D**

STOP

# Reading Literary Text: Drama

In this part of the book, you will read a play with instruction about the elements of drama. Following the selection are sample questions and answers about the play. The purpose of this section is to show you how to understand and analyze drama.

To begin, review the TEKS that relate to drama:

| DRAMA TEKS | WHAT IT MEANS TO YOU |
|---|---|
| **(5) Comprehension of Literary Text/Drama** Students understand, make inferences and draw conclusions about the structure and elements of drama and provide evidence from text to support their understanding. Students are expected to explain the similarities and differences in the setting, characters, and plot of a play and those in a film based upon the same story line. | You will understand and draw conclusions about the way dramas are put together and support your analysis with examples from the text. You will compare and contrast a drama with a movie version of the drama and explain how the setting, characters, and plot are similar or different in the two versions. |

The selection that follows provides instruction on the drama TEKS as well as other TEKS. It also covers reading comprehension skills, such as making inferences about text.

As you read the play *The Wolf and the House Dog,* notice how the author uses dialogue to retell a classic fable by Aesop. The annotations in the margins will guide you as you read.

# Guided Reading

Read this selection. Then answer the questions that follow.

## The Wolf and the House Dog

*You have probably heard fables by Aesop, the ancient Greek storyteller. Each brief story teaches a lesson about life. This play is based on one of Aesop's best-known fables.*

### Characters

Narrator

Wolf

House Dog

**Narrator.** Once there was a Wolf who never got enough to eat. Her mouth watered when she looked at the fat geese and chickens kept by the people of the village. But every time she tried to steal one, the watchful village
5  dogs would bark and warn their owners.

**Wolf.** Really, I'm nothing but skin and bones. It makes me sad just thinking about it.

**Narrator.** One night the Wolf met up with a House Dog who had wandered a little too far from home. The Wolf
10  would gladly have eaten him right then and there.

**Wolf.** Dog stew . . . cold dog pie . . . or maybe just dog on a bun, with plenty of mustard and ketchup . . .

**Narrator.** But the House Dog looked too big and strong for the Wolf, who was weak from hunger. So the Wolf
15  spoke to him very humbly and politely.

**Wolf.** How handsome you are! You look so healthy and well fed and delicious—I mean, uh, terrific. You look terrific. Really.

**ELEMENTS OF DRAMA**
Some plays include a narrator, who gives the audience information that is not presented in the dialogue, or the conversation between characters. The narrator's speech in lines 1–5 explains why it is so difficult for the Wolf to find food.

**TEKS 5**

GO ON

**House Dog.** Well, you look terrible. I don't know why
20  you live out here in these miserable woods, where you
have to fight so hard for every crummy little scrap of
food. You should come live in the village like me. You
could eat like a king there.

**Wolf.** What do I have to do?

25  **House Dog.** Hardly anything. Chase kids on bicycles.
Bark at the mailman every now and then. Lie around the
house letting people pet you. Just for that they'll feed
you till you burst—enormous steak bones with fat
hanging off them, pizza crusts, bits of chicken, leftovers
30  like you wouldn't believe.

**Narrator.** The Wolf nearly cried with happiness as she
imagined how wonderful her new life was going to be.
But then she noticed a strange ring around the Dog's
neck where the hair had been rubbed off.

35  **Wolf.** What happened to your neck?

**House Dog.** Oh . . . ah . . . nothing. It's nothing, really.

**Wolf.** I've never seen anything like it. Is it a disease?

**House Dog.** Don't be silly. It's just the mark of the
collar that they fasten my chain to.

40  **Wolf.** A chain! You mean you can't go wherever
you like?

**House Dog.** Well, not always. But what's the difference?

**Wolf.** What's the difference? Are you kidding? I wouldn't
give up my freedom for the biggest, juiciest steak in the
45  world. Never mind a few lousy bones.

**Narrator.** The Wolf ran away, back to the woods. She
never went near the village again, no matter how hungry
she got.

**All Together.** Nothing is worth more than freedom.

---

**SENSORY LANGUAGE**
Writers use language that appeals to the senses. In lines 28–29, the phrase "enormous steak bones with fat hanging off them" shows you what the House Dog eats and helps you see more clearly the contrast between the lives of the two characters.

**TEKS 8**

**ELEMENTS OF DRAMA**
In drama, new problems often arise just when the character's struggle, or conflict, appears to be over. Before the Wolf hears the Dog's explanation of the ring around his neck, she thinks her conflict might be solved. Notice how new information in lines 35–39 complicates her decision.

**TEKS 5**

**THEME**
The theme or message of a literary work might be directly stated, or it might be implied. In this play, the theme is stated in the last line of dialogue, which is spoken by all of the characters together.

**TEKS 3A**

Name _____ Date _____

**1** From the description of the Wolf as "skin and bones" in line 6, you can tell that —

**A** wolves are naturally thinner than dogs

**B** the Wolf will be forced to eat the House Dog

**C** wolves are not meant to live in the wild

**D** the Wolf has had a hard life

**EXPLANATION:** The phrase means that the Wolf is painfully thin as the result of going without food for a long period of time. **D** is correct.
- **A** and **C** are incorrect. A general statement about all wolves cannot be based on a description of just one.
- **B** is incorrect. This phrase gives no clue about the Wolf's future actions.

**TEKS 8; Fig. 19D**

**2** The narrator alone tells the audience —

**F** what the House Dog gets to eat

**G** why the Wolf does not make a meal of the House Dog

**H** what happens to the House Dog after the play ends

**J** the moral of the play

**EXPLANATION:** The narrator supplies details that do not come out through dialogue. In lines 13–15, the narrator states that the Wolf is too weak from hunger to attack the healthy and strong House Dog. **G** is correct.
- **F** is incorrect. The House Dog himself describes his daily menu.
- **H** is incorrect. The narrator explains that the Wolf never goes near the village again, but leaves it up to the audience to figure out that the House Dog goes home.
- **J** is incorrect. The theme is stated by all of the characters at the end of the play.

**TEKS 5**

**3** If the Wolf had not seen the ring around the House Dog's neck, she would have —

**A** remained friends with the House Dog

**B** attacked the House Dog

**C** moved to the village

**D** stayed in the woods

> **EXPLANATION:** The narrator says that "the Wolf nearly cried with happiness as she imagined how wonderful her new life was going to be." This statement shows that she had decided to move to the village before she saw the ring around the Dog's neck. Therefore, **C** is correct.
> - **A** is incorrect. There is no evidence to show that the two characters are friends to begin with.
> - **B** is incorrect. The Wolf already knows that she is too weak to attack the House Dog.
> - **D** is incorrect. The Wolf stays in the woods *after* she learns of the collar and chain.

**TEKS 5; Fig. 19D**

**4** Which of the following is an example of hyperbole in the play?

**F** *Once there was a wolf who never got enough to eat.*

**G** *Just for that they'll feed you till you burst. . . .*

**H** *It's just the mark of the collar that they fasten my chain to.*

**J** *Nothing is worth more than freedom.*

> **EXPLANATION:** Hyperbole means exaggeration for literary effect. **G** is correct. The House Dog uses exaggeration to show how well fed he is in the village.
> - **F** and **H** are incorrect. These statements are factual, not exaggerated.
> - **J** is incorrect. Although it is a bold statement, it is true, at least for the Wolf, who would rather starve than be chained.

**TEKS 8**

**5** Based on what the House Dog says throughout the play, what does he value more than freedom?

**A** Independence

**B** Loyalty

**C** Security

**D** Justice

> **EXPLANATION:** The theme, or message, of the play is revealed through the contrast of the two characters' choices. Although the Wolf is willing to suffer for the sake of freedom, the House Dog prefers the security of his confined existence. **C** is correct.
> - **A** is incorrect. The House Dog fears the hardships that come with independence.
> - **B** is incorrect. It is not clear that the House Dog feels loyal to his human owners. Rather, he is portrayed as simply enjoying the benefits of living with them.
> - **D** is incorrect. There is no evidence that the House Dog cares about justice.

**TEKS 5**

# Reading Informational Text: Expository Text

In this part of the book, you will read an informational article with instruction about the elements of expository text. Following the selection are sample questions and answers about the article. The purpose of this section is to show you how to understand and analyze expository text.

To begin, review the TEKS that relate to expository text:

| EXPOSITORY TEXT TEKS | WHAT IT MEANS TO YOU |
|---|---|
| **(10) Comprehension of Informational Text/Expository Text** Students analyze, make inferences and draw conclusions about expository text and provide evidence from text to support their understanding. Students are expected to: | |
| (A) summarize the main ideas and supporting details in text, demonstrating an understanding that a summary does not include opinions; | You will summarize the main idea of a text and the details that support the main idea. Your summary will only include facts from the text, not your personal opinions. |
| (B) explain whether facts included in an argument are used for or against an issue; | You will tell the difference between facts that are used to argue for an issue and facts used to argue against an issue. |
| (C) explain how different organizational patterns (e.g., proposition-and-support, problem-and-solution) develop the main idea and the author's viewpoint; and | You will explain how authors organize their writing in different ways, such as proposition-and-support or problem-and-solution, to express their views and main ideas. |
| (D) synthesize and make logical connections between ideas within a text and across two or three texts representing similar or different genres. | You will make connections between the ideas found in one text and similar ideas found in different kinds of texts. |

The selection that follows provides instruction on the expository text TEKS as well as other TEKS. It also covers reading comprehension skills, such as summarizing and making inferences about text.

As you read the article "Wolf Communication," notice the author's main idea and the details that support it. The annotations in the margins will guide you as you read.

Name _____ Date _____

# Guided Reading

> **Read this selection. Then answer the questions that follow.**

## Wolf Communication

1    The Big Bad Wolf who threatened the three little pigs . . . the wolf who disguised himself as a grandmother and ate Little Red Riding Hood . . . the story of the little shepherd boy who cried "Wolf!" . . . a lone wolf howling in the moonlight—all these familiar images of the wolf have one thing in common: they give a false picture. Contrary to stereotypes born out of human fear, the wolf is not a cold-blooded killer of humans, nor is it a solitary hunter. In fact, wolves are very family- and pack-oriented and have a rich social life, which they maintain by communicating with each other in a variety of interesting ways. These wolf communication behaviors include facial contact, howling, and scent marking.

2    Facial contact behaviors, the most intimate type of wolf communication, closely resemble what humans do when they nuzzle their babies or hug and kiss one another as a greeting. Wolves use nose pushing, cheek rubbing, facial licking, and jaw wrestling to greet one another, to give a friendly welcome, or sometimes to show dominance. For example, jaw wrestling—a behavior in which two wolves mouth one another's jaws—can be a greeting or it can be a way of intimidating a lower-ranking wolf. If one wolf puts its mouth over another's muzzle, it is giving a sign of friendship. But if the first wolf has its teeth bared, the greeting is not so friendly—it is the wolf's way of establishing itself as the more dominant, or more important, member of the wolf pack.

3    Howling is another important way that wolves communicate. You may think that wolves howl because they are lonely, but in fact they usually howl for social purposes. Barry Lopez, author of the book *Of Wolves and Men,* says that wolves probably don't howl during a chase but often do howl after a hunt, "perhaps to celebrate a successful hunt (the presence of food), their

### ELEMENTS OF EXPOSITORY TEXT
In paragraph 1, the writer presents a proposition, or main idea, about wolves. As you read further, look for details that support this idea.

**TEKS 10C, 10D**

### CONTEXT CLUES
If the word *intimate* in paragraph 2 is unfamiliar to you, the types of behaviors it describes will give you a clue to its meaning. Nose pushing, cheek rubbing, and licking help you figure out that *intimate* means "personal, or involving close contact."

**TEKS 2B**

### AUTHOR'S PURPOSE
A writer's purpose is revealed by the details that he or she chooses to include. Think about why the writer included this explanation of wolves' howling in paragraph 3.

**TEKS 9**

GO ON

prowess, or the fact that they are all together again, that no one has been injured." Wolves howl often during breeding and courtship times (in the winter), and more often in the evening or early morning. However, contrary to popular belief, they don't howl at the moon, and they don't howl any more often when there is a full moon.

4  Wolves also communicate by scent marking. Wolves leave scent marks to define their territory, as if to erect an invisible fence that only other wolves with their keen sense of smell can detect. They mark their territory partly for the same reasons that we put our names and initials on our books, mailboxes, sweaters, bracelets—to say, "This is mine." Scent marks help a wolf to know if it is in its own territory. They may even keep a pack together. To leave scent marks, wolves scratch the ground every few minutes as they are traveling. And wolves on the move stop every few minutes to inspect scent marks left by other wolves.

**SUPPORTING DETAILS**
Details in paragraph 4 help to support and elaborate on the writer's proposition in paragraph 1.
**TEKS 10C, 10D**

5  The more we learn about these and other forms of wolf communication, the better we understand the complex social structure of wolf packs. Perhaps by gaining insight into these magnificent animals—who form enduring relationships, just as humans do—we can learn more about ourselves and our place in the world of nature.

**MAKING INFERENCES**
When you infer, you combine evidence from the text with your prior knowledge. From the ideas and language in the conclusion (paragraph 5), you can infer what the writer feels, and wants others to think, about wolves.
**Fig. 19D**

**Use "Wolf Communication" (pp. 27–28) to answer questions 1–6.**

**1** Which statement is the best summary of this selection?

**A** Wolves are magnificent animals that are routinely misunderstood and mistreated by humans.

**B** Nose pushing, cheek rubbing, and jaw wrestling are important ways in which wolves communicate.

**C** Wolves are social creatures who communicate through facial contact, howling, and scent marking.

**D** Many folk tales and other stories portray wolves as bloodthirsty and scary creatures.

**EXPLANATION:** A summary includes the main idea and most important details of a selection. It does not include opinions. The main idea of this selection is that wolves are social creatures who communicate with each other. The selection then explains three important ways in which they do so. **C** is correct.

• **A** is incorrect because it is an opinion rather than a summary of the information in the selection.

• **B** is incorrect because the statement summarizes only one type of communication that wolves use.

• **D** is incorrect because it expresses only one detail from the selection.

**TEKS 10A; Fig. 19E**

**2** Another word for enduring in paragraph 5 is —

**F** lasting
**G** difficult
**H** temporary
**J** happy

**EXPLANATION:** The selection emphasizes that wolves maintain relationships among their family and pack members. Their relationships endure, or last. **F** is correct.

• **G** and **J** are incorrect. These definitions are not supported by any context clues or details earlier in the selection.

• **H** is incorrect. This word is the opposite of what the details in the selection indicate about wolves' relationships.

**TEKS 2B**

**GO ON**

**3** What is the author's primary purpose in this selection?

   **A** To make readers appreciate the important qualities of wolves

   **B** To compare wolves with other pack animals

   **C** To explain why wolves howl

   **D** To encourage policies that offer protection for wolves and other wild animals

**EXPLANATION:** Details in the text, such as the positive comparisons between humans and wolves, reveal that the author's purpose is to reduce the audience's fear of wolves and make them seem more sympathetic to readers. **A** is correct.
- **B** is incorrect. No other pack animals are mentioned in the selection.
- **C** is incorrect. The explanation of howling is just one part of the selection.
- **D** is incorrect. An indirect result of making readers more sympathetic to wolves might be to get them involved in preservation efforts, but that is not the author's purpose.

**TEKS 9; Fig. 19D**

**4** Which detail supports the idea that wolves may have human-like emotions?

   **F** They jaw wrestle to establish dominance.

   **G** They use scent marks to define the pack's territory.

   **H** They have a complex social structure.

   **J** Their howling after a hunt may be a form of celebration.

**EXPLANATION:** The quotation from Barry Lopez's book, about wolves' post-hunt howling, supports the idea that they feel pride, joy, and relief just as humans do. **J** is correct.
- **F** and **G** are incorrect. Although they are accurate facts about wolves' behavior, they do not support the idea that wolves have any particular emotions.
- **H** is incorrect. It is not a supporting detail. It is a conclusion, and it doesn't relate to human emotions.

**TEKS 10C, 10D; Fig. 19D**

**5** Which of the following best describes the overall organization of the selection?

**A** The writer explains the causes and effects of wolf behaviors.

**B** The writer describes human social behaviors and compares them to similar behaviors of wolves.

**C** The writer states a proposition about wolves and provides details to support that view.

**D** The writer examines popular stories about wolves and explains why each one is untrue.

**EXPLANATION:** In the first paragraph, the writer states the main idea that wolves are not cold-blooded killers but family-oriented creatures. The writer then goes on to support this proposition with specific and relevant details. Therefore, **C** is correct.
- **A** is incorrect. The writer does explain the reasons behind some wolf behaviors but does not explore the effects beyond saying that they are ways of communication.
- **B** is incorrect. The selection includes some comparisons between humans and wolves, but the overall organization is not comparison and contrast.
- **D** is incorrect. In the introduction and in paragraph 3, the writer briefly mentions some false stories associated with wolves, but this does not affect the organization of the selection.

**TEKS 10C**

**6** Read the chart below.

| Humans | Wolves |
|---|---|
| Greet each other by hugging or kissing | Greet each other by nose pushing or cheek rubbing |
| Put their names on their possessions | Leave scent markers |
| Form and maintain relationships | Are family- and pack-oriented |
| **Conclusion:** _____ | |

Which statement belongs on the blank line?

**F** Wolves are among the most advanced of wild animals.

**G** Humans and wolves have more in common than people might think.

**H** All wild animals have good reasons for what they do.

**J** Humans and wolves are the most alike of all species of mammals.

**EXPLANATION:** The chart shows similarities between humans and wolves. Therefore, a logical conclusion based upon these details is that humans and wolves are similar in surprising ways. **G** is correct. **F, H,** and **J** are incorrect because none of these conclusions is supported by the details in the chart.

**TEKS 10D; Fig. 19D**

STOP

# Reading Informational Text: Persuasive Text

In this part of the book, you will read a short letter with instruction about persuasive text. Following the selection are sample questions and answers about the letter. The purpose of this section is to show you how to understand and analyze the characteristics of persuasive text.

To begin, review the TEKS that relate to persuasive text:

| PERSUASIVE TEXT TEKS | WHAT IT MEANS TO YOU |
| --- | --- |
| **(11) Comprehension of Informational Text/Persuasive Text** Students analyze, make inferences and draw conclusions about persuasive text and provide evidence from text to support their analysis. Students are expected to: | |
| (A) compare and contrast the structure and viewpoints of two different authors writing for the same purpose, noting the stated claim and supporting evidence; and | You will compare and contrast the way two authors write with the same goal in mind and pay attention to the claims and supporting evidence used by each author. |
| (B) identify simple faulty reasoning used in persuasive texts. | You will identify when poor reasoning is used as support in persuasive texts. |

The selection that follows provides instruction on the persuasive text TEKS as well as other TEKS. It also covers reading comprehension skills, such as synthesizing and summarizing ideas in text.

As you read the letter "Uniform Style," notice how the speaker organizes and supports the argument. The annotations in the margins will guide you as you read.

# Guided Reading

---

**Read this selection. Then answer the questions that follow.**

---

## Uniform Style

*A student wrote this letter to the editor of her local newspaper. In it, she argues in favor of students wearing uniforms in public schools.*

1    Why are more and more public schools in the United States considering uniforms? "It's the whole issue of setting a tone for the day," says Mary Marquez, an elementary school principal in a California school district that recently made uniforms mandatory. "When students are in their uniforms, they know they are going to school to learn, not going outside to play."

2    If dressing in the latest fashions makes kids feel hip and cool, does wearing a school uniform make them feel more like serious students? Many teachers and principals say yes. They believe that uniforms encourage their students to live up to higher standards and that they promote school spirit, discipline, and academic excellence.

3    But what about the right to individuality, creativity, and expression? That's what some civil liberties[1] experts are concerned about, and many students and parents agree. Some have even gone so far as to bring lawsuits against schools that won't let students wear what they like.

**ROOTS AND AFFIXES**
Understanding word parts can help you figure out word meanings. In paragraph 1, the word *mandatory* is formed from the word *mandate,* meaning "command." The suffix *-ory* means "of or relating to." *Mandatory* means "required."

**TEKS 2A**

**ELEMENTS OF PERSUASIVE TEXT**
In paragraph 3, the author describes an opposing viewpoint on the issue of school uniforms. Compare the reasons supporting this claim (that students should not have to wear uniforms) with the reasons supporting the author's claim.

**TEKS 11A**

---

1. **civil liberties:** rights guaranteed to all citizens by the laws of a country. The U.S. Constitution guarantees freedom of speech, which protects citizens' rights to share information, ideas, and opinions.

**GO ON ➤**

4    Still, many parents, tired of spending money month after month to buy trendy clothing for their children, are only too pleased to have uniforms settle the question once and for all. Many students also welcome an end to clothing competition. "I don't worry about what I wear in the morning," says a twelve-year-old uniform wearer. "I just slip on the clothes." Students from wealthy families no longer show off their expensive clothes at school, and students who can't afford them won't face being teased about the way they dress. Of course, buying school uniforms can be hard on the pocketbook as well. However, a number of schools have started programs to help parents pay for them.

5    Some of the statements made by supporters of uniforms may seem exaggerated—for example, how could requiring students to dress alike make public schools safer? But there are logical arguments to back up this claim. Fights are less likely to break out over a leather jacket or a $150 pair of sneakers if no one is wearing such items to school. Those who don't belong on school grounds stand out among students wearing school uniforms.

6    In one California district, statistics tell the story: School crime went down 36 percent after students began wearing uniforms. Fighting dropped 51 percent and vandalism 18 percent. Other districts that began requiring uniforms report similar improvements.

7    In public school districts across the country, the jury is still out on the question of school uniforms. But with so many possible benefits for our own school, I say, why not give uniforms a try?

**PERSUASIVE TECHNIQUE**
A testimonial is a persuasive technique that relies on the opinion of a well-known person, an expert, or a satisfied customer. In paragraph 4, the author provides the testimonial of a student who supports school uniforms.

**TEKS 13C**

**FAULTY REASONING**
Exaggeration is an example of faulty reasoning that weakens an argument. In paragraph 5, the author admits that some of the claims made about uniforms do seem exaggerated. However, the author provides evidence in paragraphs 5 and 6 to support the claims about safety.

**TEKS 11B**

GO ON ➡

Name _____ Date _____

Use "Uniform Style" (pp. 33–34) to answer questions 1–6.

**1** Which of the following best describes the persuasive technique used in paragraph 1?

**A** The author relies on the testimonial of a school principal who supports uniforms.

**B** The author suggests that readers should be angry about underperforming schools.

**C** The author reasons that all schools should require uniforms because others do.

**D** The author exaggerates the effect school uniforms have in helping students focus on their schoolwork.

**EXPLANATION:** In paragraph 1, the author provides the principal's quotation as support for the idea of school uniforms. **A** is correct.
- **B** is incorrect. The quotation suggests that uniforms encourage elementary students to focus on schoolwork, but it does not suggest that readers should be angry about underperformance.
- **C** is incorrect. While the author notes that uniforms have become popular with schools, she does not attempt to use a "bandwagon" appeal to suggest that this is a reason for others to adopt the policy.
- **D** is incorrect. The author does not exaggerate the effectiveness of school uniforms in helping students focus on their work.

TEKS 11B, 13C

**2** Which of the following best summarizes the reasoning provided in paragraph 3 for the opposing point of view?

**F** Students have a right to decide what they want to wear.

**G** Many parents think that school uniforms are a cause for concern.

**H** Schools have been challenged in court over the issue of uniforms.

**J** Civil liberties experts feel that uniforms make it hard for students to communicate.

**EXPLANATION:** The reasoning against school uniforms is that students' right to individuality, creativity, and expression includes their right to choose what they will wear. **F** is correct.
- **G** is incorrect. While paragraph 3 mentions parents' concern about uniforms, this is not the main reason presented in the text.
- **H** is incorrect. Paragraph 3 mentions lawsuits against schools, but the reasoning behind the lawsuits is the main point.
- **J** is incorrect. Opponents of school uniforms argue that students are denied their right to express themselves through their clothing, but uniforms would not make it difficult for them to communicate in other ways.

TEKS 11A; Fig. 19E

GO ON

**3** Read the following dictionary entry.

> **expression** \ĭk sprĕsh´ ən\ *n.*
> **1.** communication in words, art, music, or movement  **2.** a particular phrase or saying  **3.** a facial look that conveys a feeling  **4.** the act of pressing or squeezing out

What is the definition of <u>expression</u> as it is used in paragraph 3?

**A** Definition 1

**B** Definition 2

**C** Definition 3

**D** Definition 4

**EXPLANATION: A** is correct. *Expression* is the act of expressing, or communicating information, ideas, or opinions through speaking, showing, or performing. Context clues tell you that *expression* relates to *individuality* and *creativity,* and opponents of uniforms argue that prohibiting students from choosing their own clothing denies them these rights.
- **B** and **D** are incorrect. These definitions do not make sense when substituted for *expression* in paragraph 3.
- **C** is incorrect. Although it's possible to discuss a person's right to have a certain look on his or her face, the context is about clothing, not facial expressions.

**TEKS 2A, 2B, 2E**

**4** The reasoning in paragraph 4 supports the conclusion that uniforms —

**F** are uncomfortable for many students

**G** are more expensive than other clothes

**H** promote a sense of equality among students

**J** encourage more parents to get involved in their children's schools

**EXPLANATION:** The reasoning in this paragraph suggests that clothing competition is an issue at schools, and mandatory school uniforms do away with that competition. This supports the conclusion that uniforms help promote a sense of equality among students. **H** is correct.
- **F** is incorrect. The author provides examples and quotes to show students' support of uniforms.
- **G** is incorrect. While the author acknowledges that purchasing uniforms can be expensive, there is no evidence to suggest that uniforms are more expensive than other clothes.
- **J** is incorrect. The text says nothing about parent involvement at schools.

**TEKS 11; Fig. 19E**

GO ON ➡

**5** The supporting evidence the author provides in paragraph 6 is best described as —

**A** a testimonial

**B** a set of statistics

**C** an emotional appeal

**D** a bandwagon appeal

**EXPLANATION:** Statistics are evidence in the form of numbers. "School crime went down 36 percent after students began wearing uniforms" is a statistic from a study on school crime rates. The author provides two additional statistics in the paragraph. **B** is correct.

- **A** is incorrect. The author does not provide any quotations in this paragraph.
- **C** is incorrect. The author does not appeal to strong feelings such as anger or pity. This answer is also incorrect because emotional appeals are a persuasive technique, not a kind of evidence.
- **D** is incorrect. The author does not suggest that people should support uniforms to fit in with others, and bandwagon appeals are a persuasive technique rather than supporting evidence.

**TEKS 11, 13C**

**6** Which of the following best describes the overall structure of the text?

**F** The author provides a series of strong reasons for adopting school uniforms, then proposes that her school should adopt them.

**G** The author claims that her school should adopt a uniform policy, then gives reasons.

**H** The author provides a fairly equal number of views for and against uniforms, then gives her own view.

**J** The author explores the pros and cons of uniforms but does not put forward a proposal.

**EXPLANATION:** The author provides several reasons for and against school uniforms, then proposes that her school should adopt them. **H** is correct.

- **F** is incorrect. The author gives multiple viewpoints on uniforms, not just those in favor.
- **G** is incorrect. The author does not reveal her viewpoint on uniforms until the end of the letter.
- **J** is incorrect. In the final paragraph of the letter, the author proposes that her school adopt a uniform policy.

**TEKS 11**

STOP

# Reading Informational and Literary Text: Paired Selections

In this part of the book, you will read two selections: an informational article with instruction about the elements of expository text, and a short story with instruction about the elements of fiction. Following the selections are sample questions and answers about the two pieces. The purpose of this section is to show you how to understand and analyze selections from two different genres and how to compare and contrast them.

To begin, review the TEKS that relate to expository text and fiction:

| EXPOSITORY TEXT TEKS | WHAT IT MEANS TO YOU |
| --- | --- |
| **(10) Comprehension of Informational Text/Expository Text** Students analyze, make inferences and draw conclusions about expository text and provide evidence from text to support their understanding. Students are expected to: | |
| (A) summarize the main ideas and supporting details in text, demonstrating an understanding that a summary does not include opinions; | You will summarize the main idea of a text and the details that support the main idea. Your summary will only include facts from the text, not your personal opinions. |
| (B) explain whether facts included in an argument are used for or against an issue; | You will tell the difference between facts that are used to argue for an issue and facts used to argue against an issue. |
| (C) explain how different organizational patterns (e.g., proposition-and-support, problem-and-solution) develop the main idea and the author's viewpoint; and | You will explain how authors organize their writing in different ways, such as proposition-and-support or problem-and-solution, to express their views and main ideas. |
| (D) synthesize and make logical connections between ideas within a text and across two or three texts representing similar or different genres. | You will make connections between the ideas found in one text and similar ideas found in different kinds of texts. |

| FICTION TEKS | WHAT IT MEANS TO YOU |
| --- | --- |
| **(6) Comprehension of Literary Text/Fiction** Students understand, make inferences and draw conclusions about the structure and elements of fiction and provide evidence from text to support their understanding. Students are expected to: | |
| (A) summarize the elements of plot development (e.g., rising action, turning point, climax, falling action, denouement) in various works of fiction; | You will explain the different parts of a plot, including rising action, turning point, climax, falling action, and denouement, in a story. |
| (B) recognize dialect and conversational voice and explain how authors use dialect to convey character; and | You will recognize dialect (language spoken in a particular area or by a particular group) and discuss how authors portray their characters through speech. |
| (C) describe different forms of point-of-view, including first- and third-person. | You will understand the different points of view from which a story is told, including first-person and third-person point of view. |

The selections that follow provide instruction on the expository text TEKS, the fiction TEKS, and other TEKS. They also cover reading comprehension skills, such as summarizing and making inferences about text.

As you read the article "Let the Chips Fall" and the story "A Valuable Lesson," notice how the authors use the elements described in the charts on page 38. Notice also the similarities and differences in structure and meaning between the story and the article. The annotations in the margins will guide you as you read.

© Houghton Mifflin Harcourt Publishing Company

# Guided Reading

**Read the next two selections. Then answer the questions that follow.**

## Let the Chips Fall

1   For a chef, the worst disaster is when a recipe fails. The second worst disaster is when a customer doesn't like the food. Yet, thanks to a picky customer and a hot-tempered chef, we have the potato chip. The next time you bite into a chip, think about George Crum. He's the chef who invented that salty, tasty little snack. Here's how it happened.

2   Back in 1853, Chef Crum worked at Moon Lake Lodge. This was a fancy <u>resort</u> in Saratoga County, New York. The resort served the richest people on the East Coast. They acted like kings and queens. They wanted things done their way and only their way.

3   Crum, who was part Native American and part African American, was proud of his cooking. He also had a temper like a volcano. If someone didn't like his food, he didn't just give them something else. He would make something so awful that the person might even get up and leave the lodge.

4   Like many chefs, Crum offered French fries as part of the menu. People had loved French fries ever since Thomas Jefferson's day. Mr. Jefferson had brought the recipe back from France. One day, an important customer came into Moon Lake Lodge to eat. Some people say it was Cornelius "Commodore" Vanderbilt, a famous millionaire. He tasted Chef Crum's French fries and scowled. To him the fries were like sponges—not crunchy enough. He sent them back to the kitchen.

5   Chef Crum's temper was heating up. *Not crunchy enough? We'll see about that.* The chef cooked another batch of fries and sent them out to Vanderbilt.

6   The Commodore tasted one, and then shook his head. The fries still weren't crunchy enough. Back they went to the kitchen.

### MAIN IDEA

The main idea of a nonfiction work is the most important idea that the author wants to communicate. From this first paragraph, you learn that the potato chip was invented by George Crum under interesting circumstances. As you read, look for supporting details that explain these circumstances.

**TEKS 10A**

### CONTEXT CLUES

To define an unfamiliar word, such as *scowled* in paragraph 4, look for clues in the sentences around it. After Vanderbilt scowls, he sends back the fries because he does not like them. From this action, you can infer that *scowled* means "made a facial expression that showed displeasure."

**TEKS 2B**

GO ON →

7    When Chef Crum saw the plate, he finally exploded. *I'll show that Vanderbilt a thing or two!* He sliced another batch of potatoes as thin as paper. You could almost see through each slice. He fried the potatoes until they were golden and crispy. You couldn't eat these fries with a fork—they would break. Crum was sure that Vanderbilt would hate them.

8    The Commodore loved the paper-thin chips. He ate every one and asked for another batch, and then another. Without meaning to, Chef Crum had invented a new snack food—the potato chip.

9    Soon everyone at the lodge began asking for these new potato chips. At first, Chef Crum called them "potato crunches." After a while, they showed up on the menu as "Saratoga Chips."

10    The chef's "disaster" turned out to be one of the best things that ever happened to him. When Crum opened his own restaurant, he placed baskets of chips on each table. He even sold the chips in boxes for people to take home. (By the way, some people say that Vanderbilt helped Crum open his new restaurant!)

11    Soon potato chips were showing up in restaurants all over the country. Then someone decided to put them in bags and sell them to grocery stores. By 1929 a new fryer was invented that could fry chips by the hundreds. Now people could ship thousands of bags of chips from coast to coast.

12    Today, potato chips are the most popular snack food in America. They come in many flavors—cheese, barbeque, hot pepper, onion, vinegar, and more. We have Chef George Crum (and maybe Vanderbilt) to thank for this crunchy snack!

**AUTHOR'S PURPOSE**
The italicized sentence in paragraph 7 shows what Chef Crum might be thinking after the second plate of fries is sent back. The author includes this sentence to help you understand more clearly Chef Crum's determination to get back at his fussy customer.

**TEKS 9**

**MAKING INFERENCES**
When you make an inference, you combine details in the text with your own knowledge to understand something the author does not state directly. Using the information in parentheses in paragraph 10, you can infer that Vanderbilt and Crum settled their conflict with each other and may even have become friends.

**Fig. 19D**

GO ON ➡

## Who's Got the Best Chipping Potatoes?

13 Where do the best "chip" potatoes come from? Not from Idaho or Maine—the country's best potato states. Believe it or not, Pennsylvania grows the number one chipping potatoes in the nation. Over 70 percent of Pennsylvania's potato crop is turned into crispy chips. Other potatoes are too small, too tough, or too much in demand for other uses.

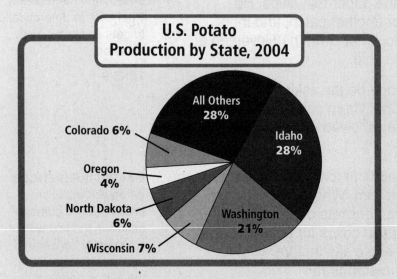

**U.S. Potato Production by State, 2004**

- All Others 28%
- Idaho 28%
- Washington 21%
- Wisconsin 7%
- North Dakota 6%
- Oregon 4%
- Colorado 6%

Although Pennsylvania grows the best potatoes for making potato chips, it is not one of the nation's top six potato-producing states.

**INTERPRETING CHARTS**
A pie chart shows the fractions or percentages that make up the whole amount of something. Consider how the information in the pie chart relates to the information in paragraph 13.

**TEKS 12B, 13A**

GO ON

# A Valuable Lesson

1    "Two cups of coffee, a bagel with cream cheese, and a hot pretzel." It was a typical order at the snack bar at the citywide garage sale my parents helped run every April. The event was supposed to raise money for the local playground. Every year we made enough money to make some improvement. This was my first year at the snack bar, though, and I was worried that instead of raising money, I would end up owing it.

2    We got to the firehouse early to set everything up. Usually, people set up tables and sell their "treasures" outside. But because the weather that day was rainy and cold, we moved inside. We set up in the garage where the fire trucks were usually parked. Without them, the room seemed huge, with a sky-high ceiling and a smooth, gray cement floor. Our voices and footsteps echoed off the bare walls and floor and sounded unfamiliar and loud.

3    . I was carrying boxes when my mother told me to fill in at the snack bar because one of the workers had the flu. I protested. I said, "No way. I'll mess it up. You know I'm no good with money, and I'll never remember the orders. Please, Mom, don't make me."

4    "Nonsense. You can do it. Besides, you won't get much business until lunch," said my mother, "and then I'll help you." I shrugged my shoulders and scraped the sole of my wet sneaker against the cement floor, making a loud squeak. I thought the idea was a bad one, but I went.

5    My mother was completely wrong. Because the weather was bad, people wanted hot snacks and drinks. I was swamped with orders. At first, I was really slow at taking the orders and making change. The line of people grew, and everybody seemed impatient. I was so nervous that my hands shook, and I spilled orange juice on the floor. What a sticky mess! Then Ms. Munoz, my math teacher, showed me how to make change by counting up to the total amount I was given. If someone gave me five dollars for something that cost $3.25,

**POINT OF VIEW**
The narrator is the voice that tells a story. This story has a first-person narrator, as you can tell from the use of the pronouns *I, we,* and *my* in paragraph 1. First-person point of view means that the narrator is a character in the story who shares what he or she sees, thinks, and feels.

**TEKS 6C**

**SENSORY LANGUAGE**
In paragraph 2, the author's use of sensory language, or words that appeal to the senses, helps you "see" the setting of the story.

**TEKS 8; Fig. 19C**

**PLOT**
The action in a story comes from the conflict, or struggle between opposing forces. This conflict may be external, between a character and an outside force. It may also be internal, or within a character. In paragraph 5, the narrator experiences both types of conflict.

**TEKS 6A**

 GO ON

I handed over three quarters and a dollar and said, "Seventy-five cents makes four dollars, plus one dollar makes five." Things went more smoothly after that. In fact, I actually started having fun.

6      A girl from my class showed up, a girl I had liked since sixth grade. At first I was terrified. What if I made a fool of myself in front of her—giving someone the wrong change or spilling another drink? "Hey, Jimmy," she said when she got to the front of the line, "can I have an orange juice, please?" My hand trembled a little as I poured the orange juice, but then I realized—I can do this! After that, I felt relaxed enough to joke around with her. She flashed me a smile before she left.

7      By the end of the day, I could pour hot coffee, slice a bagel, add up the bill, and make change quickly with a smile. I was even a little disappointed when the sun came out and dried up business. My mom said that she was proud of me, and when she suggested that I work the snack bar again next year, I did not even shrug. I was too busy imagining the restaurant I would open one day.

**TOPIC AND THEME**
The topic of a story is what it is about—for example, meeting a challenge. The theme is what the author wants to say about the topic. It's the story's lesson or message. Theme is revealed through events and their effect on the main character. Consider what theme the details in paragraph 6 suggest.

**TEKS 3A**

**MAKING CONNECTIONS**
What you read becomes more meaningful if you make connections between different texts. Think about the ways in which the narrator in this story and the chef in the previous selection are the same and different.

**TEKS 10D; Fig. 19F**

Name _____ Date _____

**Use "Let the Chips Fall" (pp. 40–42) to answer questions 1–5.**

**1** Which of these statements best summarizes the key ideas of the selection?

**A** Chef Crum worked at Moon Lake Lodge until he opened his own restaurant. He put baskets of potato chips on his tables. People loved them.

**B** The invention of a new fryer revolutionized the potato chip industry. Soon people all over the country could buy potato chips.

**C** Commodore Vanderbilt was a fussy man. He did not like Chef Crum's fries. He liked Chef Crum's potato chips, however, and later helped him open his own restaurant.

**D** Chef Crum invented the potato chip accidentally, trying to get rid of a picky customer. Unexpectedly, the customer and everyone else loved his chips. They became a popular national snack.

**EXPLANATION:** A summary states the key ideas from a selection in the correct order. **D** is correct. The selection explains how Chef Crum invented the potato chip and how it became the most popular snack food in America.
- **A** is incorrect because it overlooks the main idea of the selection, which is how the chip was invented.
- **B** is incorrect because it summarizes only the last two paragraphs of the selection.
- **C** is incorrect because the selection is not focused on Commodore Vanderbilt.

**TEKS 10A**

**2** Read the following dictionary entry.

**resort** \rĭ zôrt´\ n. **1.** the act of requesting help **2.** a place where people go for relaxation **3.** a final attempt **4.** a person who gives help

What is the definition of <u>resort</u> as it is used in paragraph 2?

**F** Definition 1
**G** Definition 2
**H** Definition 3
**J** Definition 4

**EXPLANATION:** From the context clues in paragraph 2, such as *fancy, served the richest people,* and *acted like kings and queens,* it can be inferred that a resort is an upscale vacation spot or luxury hotel. **G** is correct.
- **F** and **J** are incorrect. Context clues do not support the meanings related to asking for or giving help.
- **H** is incorrect. The resort described in this selection is not a last effort or attempt.

**TEKS 2B, 2E**

**3** Why does the author include the details in paragraphs 11 and 12?

**A** To show Americans' reliance on high-fat snacks

**B** To reinforce the importance of the invention of the potato chip

**C** To explain what happened to Chef Crum

**D** To describe the different flavors of potato chips that are now available

**EXPLANATION:** These details chart the development of the potato chip from a local specialty to a national favorite. The author includes this information to emphasize the importance of Chef Crum's invention.
**B** is correct.
- **A** is incorrect. These paragraphs contain no details about the fat content of chips or other snacks.
- **C** is incorrect. No new details about Chef Crum's life or career are included in this part of the selection.
- **D** is incorrect. The different flavors of potato chips are mentioned, but that is not the main purpose of the paragraphs.

**TEKS 9**

**4** From the behaviors of Vanderbilt and Crum, the reader can infer that both men were —

**F** friendly

**G** easygoing

**H** talented

**J** stubborn

**EXPLANATION:** Neither Chef Crum nor Commodore Vanderbilt is willing to give in. Each time Commodore Vanderbilt sends the fries back, Chef Crum sends them out again. **J** is correct. The unwillingness of either man to compromise shows their stubbornness.
- **F** is incorrect. Neither man displays qualities of friendliness in this selection.
- **G** is incorrect. If Vanderbilt were easygoing, he would have eaten the fries and not complained. If Chef Crum were easygoing, he would not have tried to make a fry that Vanderbilt did not like in return for his complaints.
- **H** is incorrect. It may be inferred from the selection that Chef Crum is talented, but it cannot be determined whether or not Vanderbilt is.

**TEKS 10D; Fig. 19D, 19F**

**5** According to paragraph 13, Maine and Pennsylvania are good places to grow potatoes. What does the information in the pie chart add to your understanding of potato growing in the United States?

**A** Most potatoes are grown in the eastern part of the United States.

**B** Although potatoes grow well in some eastern states, larger western states can grow more of them.

**C** People on the West Coast like potatoes more than people on the East Coast.

**D** Maine and Pennsylvania did not grow any potatoes in 2004.

> **EXPLANATION:** The pie chart shows the percentage of the total U.S. potato crop that was grown in various states in 2004. The two states that grew the most potatoes are Idaho and Washington, which are in the western part of the country. These states are much larger than eastern states like Maine and Pennsylvania. **B** is correct.
>
> • **A** is incorrect. None of the top six potato-producing states in the chart is in the eastern United States.
>
> • **C** is incorrect. Food can be shipped all over the world from the place where it is grown. Potatoes are produced where the soil and climate are good for growing them, not necessarily where people like to eat them.
>
> • **D** is incorrect. It is unlikely that these states would have stopped growing potatoes for one year. Maine and Pennsylvania are in the "All others" category of the chart.

**TEKS 12B, 13A**

Name _____ Date _____

**Use "A Valuable Lesson" (pp. 43–44) to answer questions 6–10.**

**6** Which descriptive phrase from the story best helps readers visualize the setting?

**F** *sticky mess*
**G** *the sun came out and dried up business*
**H** *voices and footsteps echoed off the bare walls*
**J** *my hand trembled a little*

**EXPLANATION:** Setting is where and when the story takes place. **H** is correct. This phrase helps readers visualize the vastness and emptiness of the firehouse by appealing to their senses of hearing and sight.
- **F** and **G** are incorrect. Both phrases are descriptive of particular moments but do not enhance the reader's understanding of the setting overall.
- **J** is incorrect. This phrase uses sensory language to illustrate the narrator's nervousness.

**TEKS 8**

**7** Why does the narrator shrug in paragraph 4?

**A** He is very angry at his mother.
**B** He is signaling to a friend across the room.
**C** He is showing that he will do the job but not happily.
**D** He is relaxing his shoulders.

**EXPLANATION:** The narrator's gesture in paragraph 4 is a way of saying that if everything goes wrong at the snack bar, it will be his mother's fault. This interpretation is supported by what he says at the end of the paragraph: "I thought the idea was a bad one, but I went." So, the shrug shows unwilling acceptance. **C** is correct.
- **A** is incorrect. A shrug is not a gesture of anger but rather surrender.
- **B** is incorrect. No details suggest that the narrator has a friend with whom he is communicating.
- **D** is incorrect. The last sentence of paragraph 4 indicates that the shrug is about an attitude, not physical discomfort.

**TEKS 6C; Fig. 19D**

**GO ON**

Name _____ Date _____

**8** The author chooses first-person point of view in order to —

F show the feelings of the customers as they wait in line

G reveal changes in the narrator's attitude that occur in the course of the story

H describe the mother's inner pride as she sees her son taking charge of the snack bar

J explain what the narrator's classmate thinks when she sees him

EXPLANATION: First-person point of view enables readers to learn the thoughts and feelings of the narrator. **G** is correct. The narrator says that he is disappointed at the end of the story when business at the snack bar slows down. This feeling contrasts with his earlier anxiety about taking on the job.
• **F, H,** and **J** are incorrect. The narrator does not know the thoughts and feelings of other characters in the story.

**TEKS 6C; Fig. 19D**

**9** The narrator's conflict in paragraph 5 is resolved when —

A Ms. Munoz teaches him to make change

B he spills orange juice on the cement floor

C customers become impatient

D he starts to have fun

EXPLANATION: In paragraph 5, the narrator struggles to serve customers and make change. Once he learns how to make change quickly, his day improves. **A** is correct.
• **B** is incorrect. Spilling the orange juice is another minor conflict.
• **C** is incorrect. The customers' impatience creates, rather than resolves, conflict.
• **D** is incorrect. Having fun is the result of resolving his conflict, not the actual solution.

**TEKS 6A**

**10** What valuable lesson does the narrator learn?

F How to do mental math under pressure

G How taking on a challenge can lead to self-knowledge

H How to raise money for playground equipment

J How important it is to cooperate with one's parents

EXPLANATION: The theme of this story is revealed through the actions of the narrator. Although the narrator at first sees manning the snack bar as an impossible task, he succeeds. Through the experience, he discovers that he is capable of much more than he thought. He also realizes that he would like to own a restaurant one day. **G** is correct.
• **F** is incorrect. Although the narrator learns to make change quickly, it is not the most valuable lesson he takes from his experience.
• **H** and **J** are incorrect. There is no evidence that suggests these are lessons that the narrator learns.

**TEKS 3A; Fig. 19D**

GO ON

Guided Reading
© Houghton Mifflin Harcourt Publishing Company

49

Name _____ Date _____

**Use "Let the Chips Fall" and "A Valuable Lesson" (pp. 40–44) to answer questions 11–12.**

**11** What is a major way in which Chef Crum differs from the narrator of "A Valuable Lesson"?

**A** Chef Crum has strong confidence in his abilities.

**B** Chef Crum wants to open his own restaurant.

**C** Chef Crum enjoys experimenting with new dishes.

**D** Chef Crum always wanted to be a chef.

> **EXPLANATION:** When the story opens, the narrator doubts his ability to run the snack bar. Chef Crum never doubts his abilities and refuses to compromise them to please others. He is very confident. **A** is correct.
> - **B** is incorrect. Both the chef and the narrator want to open their own restaurants.
> - **C** is incorrect. The chef does invent a new dish, but there is no evidence to suggest that this is something he enjoys doing.
> - **D** is incorrect. It is not clear from the details in the selection whether or not Chef Crum always wanted to be a chef.

**TEKS 10D; Fig. 19F**

**12** Which statement best expresses the common theme in both Chef Crum's and the narrator's experiences?

**F** Customers at a restaurant can be rude and demanding.

**G** The best inventions happen by accident.

**H** Sometimes people force you to do what you don't want to do.

**J** Negative situations can lead to positive outcomes.

> **EXPLANATION:** Both the chef and the narrator find themselves in challenging situations that seem to promise disaster. Both end up succeeding in ways that they might not have anticipated. Therefore, the message expressed in both selections is **J**. Situations that appear negative may bring about positive results.
> - **F** is incorrect. It states a fact, rather than a message about life.
> - **G** is incorrect. The narrator in the short story does not invent anything.
> - **H** is incorrect. Both Chef Crum and the narrator can be described as being forced to take certain actions. However, the statement does not express what readers can learn from observing the results of these actions.

**TEKS 3A, 10D; Fig. 19F**

STOP

# Reading Practice

Name _____ Date _____

# Reading Practice

Read this selection. Then answer the questions that follow.

## from **The Lucky Stone**

*by Lucille Clifton*

My notes about
what I am reading

*Fourteen-year-old Tee loves to sit on her front porch and
listen to her great-grandmother tell stories. Some of Tee's
favorite stories involve the history of Grandma's lucky stone,
which she plans to pass on to Tee someday.*

1    Up until the time I was fourteen years old I hadn't ever
got one valentine in the mail. And I was really worried
about having a boyfriend and all. I used to talk to my
Great-grandmother about it.

2    "Don't you worry, Sweet Tee." She would smile and
pat my plaits.[1] "They'll come round buzzin like bees to
the cone,[2] bees to the cone."

3    The year that I was going to be fourteen was the
year that she was almost eighty years old and caught
pneumonia. Oh, that scared us. She was such an old
woman. Real little and thin, but not weak-looking, just
a small old lady. She would lay in her bed watching the
sun out the window and breathing so loud seemed like
her breathing rustled the curtains.

4    After a few days Mama and Daddy wanted to take her
to the hospital, but she didn't want to go.

5    "I'll let the sun heal me," she'd fuss. "Give the sun just
one more good day."

6    "Grandmother, you need the doctor," Mama would
almost cry.

7    "The sun be my doctor if it's all right with you," my
Great-grandmother would say.

---

1. **plaits:** braids in a person's hair.
2. **like bees to the cone:** A cone is the part of a flower that produces pollen, which
attracts bees.

---

My notes about
what I am reading

8    But finally Mama and Daddy took her to the hospital.
     And every day without missing I would walk to the
     hospital with dogwood or candy and every day the nurse
     wouldn't let me see my Great-grandmother.

9    "No visitors." That's all she would say. No reason or
     nothing. No visitors.

10   Well, this one day I went over to the hospital and
     the nurse's place was empty. I didn't even think about
     it; soon as I saw nobody was there I went looking for
     my Great-grandmother. Found her too. She was in the
     fourth room I tried, a little tiny old lady in a big old bed.
     Not enough sun or nothing. I was in the room before she
     saw me.

11   "Ohhh, it's my Baby, my Sweet Tee Baby." She
     laughed. She was so glad to see me.

12   And I ran to the bed and hugged her hard because
     I was so glad to see her too. And I started to cry.

13   "Why what is the matter, Tee?"

14   "Oh, Grandma." I was talkin and cryin at the same
     time. "Grandmama, I ain't never gonna have no
     boyfriend and nobody will ever love me but you, and
     I couldn't even get in here to see you and I ain't gonna
     never have nobody."

15   My Great-grand hugged me hard.

16   "Hush your mouth, girl," she laughed, "hush up now.
     You talk like you ain't kin to me. You'll have the ones
     you want and the ones you don't. Sweet Tee, they be on
     you like bees to the cone. And you ain't done with me
     neither, not yet." And she seemed to be laughing more.

17   Well, that old nurse came in just then and made
     me go.

18   "When you get home, look on my <u>dresser</u>. Don't
     forget. Look on my dresser," my Great-grandmother
     called to me on my way out.

My notes about
what I am reading

19      That evening after my Mama and Daddy went out to
the hospital I went into my Great-grand's room and sat
in her chair. Her room smelled old and warm and sweet
like she did.

20      I went over to her dresser like she told me. I looked
at the pictures all framed in lace and gold. There were
aunts and uncles I didn't know. And Mama when she
was a little girl and Mama's Mama, my Grandmother and
my Great-grand's own daughter who was gone before
I was born.

21      And right by the picture of Mama's Mama was a
lace hanky with an envelope half folded in it. And the
envelope had my name on it! Tee!

22      I unfolded the hanky and took the envelope over to
the rocker and sat down and opened it up. There was
something inside warm and black as night, a stone with
a letter scratched on one side like an *A*. The stone!

23      Oh, I held it and kissed it and rocked and cried in
that chair and that was where they found me when they
came in that evening. My Mama and my Daddy and my
Great-grandmother well again!

24      They laughed when they saw me sitting curled up
asleep in my Great-grand's chair with the lucky stone
clutched in my hand. They say they did anyway.

25      Next day I got in the mail my very first valentine, a
big red heart edged in lace, and my Great-grandmother
laughed and called me Honeycone, and it seemed like
I smiled all day. It was the prettiest thing I had ever
seen and it was signed just J.D., and I didn't even know
that anybody called by that was looking at me when
I watched him in school so much.

26      The world is a wondrous place.

27      Now that is the story of how I got my lucky stone
and how it started being lucky for me. There is more to
it than that though, and someday I might tell you about
that too.

Name _____ Date _____

---

**Use the excerpt from *The Lucky Stone* (pp. 52–54) to answer questions 1–8.**

---

**1** From which point of view is the story told?

  **A**  First person, told by Tee's great-grandmother

  **B**  First person, told by Tee

  **C**  Third person, told by an all-knowing narrator

  **D**  Third person, told by a narrator who knows Tee's thoughts only

**2** In paragraph 2, the great-grandmother uses a simile, or comparison, involving "bees to the cone." What does she mean?

  **F**  She understands that not receiving any valentines stings or hurts Tee's feelings.

  **G**  Many boys will one day be drawn to Tee and want to be her boyfriend.

  **H**  Tee will one day be so busy that she will not worry about boyfriends.

  **J**  Tee will develop a sweeter personality as she grows older.

**3** In the South, iced tea with sugar is a popular drink called "sweet tea." What does her use of the nickname Sweet Tee convey about the great-grandmother's character?

  **A**  She is often thirsty and tries to hide this symptom of her illness.

  **B**  She comes from the North but likes eating and drinking food from the South.

  **C**  She is very well educated and likes to show off her knowledge.

  **D**  She is clever with words and feels affection for her great-granddaughter.

---

**4** The diagram below shows part of the plot's rising action, from left to right.

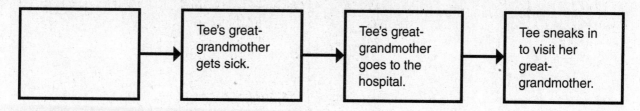

Which of the events below is missing from the first box of the diagram?

  **F**  Tee tells her great-grandmother her worries about not getting a valentine.

  **G**  Tee's great-grandmother refuses to go to the hospital.

  **H**  The nurse will not let Tee visit her great-grandmother.

  **J**  Tee gets a valentine.

---

**5** In the context of paragraph 18, what does the word <u>dresser</u> mean?

**A** Someone who helps another person put on clothing

**B** A piece of furniture

**C** A bedroom closet

**D** A machine that stamps addresses onto envelopes

**6** Which of the following is an example of dialect from the story?

**F** *After a few days Mama and Daddy wanted to take her to the hospital, but she didn't want to go.*

**G** *And I ran to the bed and hugged her hard because I was so glad to see her too.*

**H** *"Hush your mouth, girl," she laughed, "hush up now. You talk like you ain't kin to me."*

**J** *"When you get home, look on my dresser. Don't forget. Look on my dresser," my Great-grandmother called to me on my way out.*

**7** Why does the great-grandmother tell Tee where the lucky stone is?

**A** She believes she will get better if Tee brings the stone to the hospital.

**B** She is sure she is dying and wants Tee to find and inherit the stone.

**C** She wants to bring Tee luck and make Tee feel better.

**D** The stone is heart-shaped, like a valentine.

**8** Which theme, or message about life, does the story most clearly support?

**F** The love of an older family member is more valuable than romantic love.

**G** Family love and family traditions bring people comfort.

**H** The secrets of the past are often hard to understand.

**J** People make their own luck.

STOP

Name _____ Date _____

# Reading Practice

---

**Read this selection. Then answer the questions that follow.**

---

## My First Step to the White House
### by Chris Van Allsburg

My notes about
what I am reading

*Chris Van Allsburg is a writer and illustrator best known
for his books* Jumanji *and* The Polar Express. *Briefly, while
growing up in Michigan, he thought he might become
president.*

1    When I was about nine years old, my father bought
me a go-kart. It was fire-engine red and had a chain-
saw motor on the back that was a screaming terror.

2    My family lived in a neighborhood where there were
winding dirt roads, and it wasn't long before I was
blasting through turns sideways, kicking up a rooster tail
of gravel.

3    The roads weren't the only thing that was dirt. So
were the driveways. But one morning an asphalt[1] truck
pulled up to our house, and by the afternoon our dusty,
rutted drive had been <u>transformed</u> into a ribbon of
smooth black perfection, the envy of the neighborhood.

4    A few days later my mom and dad had to go out for
the afternoon. Before they left, my dad reminded me of
an agreement that we'd made: I would never, ever, use
the kart if he wasn't around. If I did, no more go-kart.

5    After my parents left, my friend Steve came over. One
thing led to another, and pretty soon we were rolling the
kart out of the garage. I figured one little ride wouldn't
hurt. Besides, my dad would never know.

6    I checked the gas tank on the kart. Empty. We
kept the extra gas in a giant ten-gallon army surplus[2]
gas can. Steve and I dragged the full can across the
driveway and lifted it up. Unfortunately, it was too heavy

---

1. **asphalt:** an oily, black substance used to pave driveways and streets.
2. **army surplus:** military goods that are sold when the army no longer needs them.

---

My notes about
what I am reading

for us. We ended up pouring one gallon into the cart and about nine gallons onto the driveway.

7    Do you know what happens to fresh asphalt when gasoline gets on it? Neither did I. It turns into a gooey black muck and sort of melts away. Steve and I stared at the crater[3] in my driveway like it was a chemistry experiment gone very wrong.

8    I knew I was in big trouble. Not only had I broken my promise about not using the go-kart, I'd also messed up our brand-new driveway. I felt so bad; I just rolled the kart back into the garage.

9    I waited for my parents to come home, feeling worse every minute. Finally, they pulled into the driveway and parked right over the hole. They hadn't noticed it. Was I lucky!

10   I knew when my dad discovered the hole, he'd ask me about it. I'd just blame it on the car. Everybody knows cars leak gas, right?

11   My mom fixed dinner, but I didn't have much of an appetite. In fact, I was starting to feel pretty bad. The idea of waiting until someone discovered the hole and then lying about it was too much for me. I couldn't take it. Before we had dessert, I dragged my dad out to the driveway and confessed. I think I may have started crying a little bit, too. My dad moved the car and looked at the hole. "Well," he said, "that's not too bad. Let's go back in and have some ice cream."

12   My dad did end up taking the kart away, but only for a few weeks. When I went to my room that night I felt pretty lucky. Lying in bed, I realized I'd heard about this sort of thing happening before. I'm sure you have heard the story, too. It's called "Parson Weems' Fable," and it tells how young George Washington cut down a cherry tree. When his father discovered the fallen tree, George said, "I cannot tell a lie, father, I did it with my little hatchet."

13   George escaped the worse punishment he might have gotten, because he'd told the truth. "Golly," I thought, "I just did that myself!" I fell asleep wondering if one day I'd be president, too.

3. **crater:** a large pit or hole.

Name _____ Date _____

**Use "My First Step to the White House" (pp. 57–58) to answer questions 1–7.**

**1** What is the author's main purpose in writing this autobiographical account?

**A** To pay tribute to his father

**B** To describe a memorable experience that helped teach him a lesson

**C** To explain the dangers of pouring gasoline on fresh asphalt

**D** To teach readers the difference between right and wrong

**2** Based on the images in paragraph 2, what can you guess about the author's activities after he got his go-kart?

**F** He was afraid to use it and drove it slowly.

**G** He sped around for a while but soon lost interest in it.

**H** He drove it quickly and with great enthusiasm.

**J** He made chicken noises as he drove around in it.

**3** Which type of figurative language does the author use when he describes the newly paved driveway as "a ribbon of smooth black perfection" (paragraph 3)?

**A** Simile

**B** Personification

**C** Hyperbole

**D** Refrain

**4** Based on the context clues in paragraph 3, what does the word <u>transform</u> mean?

**F** Change

**G** Drive

**H** Make jealous

**J** Stay the same

**5** Paragraphs 12 and 13 make an allusion, or brief reference, to a well-known legend about George Washington. What lesson do both Washington and the young Van Allsburg learn?

**A** Honesty is the best policy.

**B** Violence is never the answer.

**C** Children often misbehave when their parents are away.

**D** Anyone can grow up to be president.

**6** What is the main difference between the young boy who spills the gasoline and the older man who tells the story years later?

**F** The older man is less honest with himself.

**G** The older man is more daring and adventurous.

**H** The older man knows the story of George Washington.

**J** The older man sees the humor in the situation.

**7** Think about the structure of this autobiographical account. What role does the title play?

**A** It stresses the author's political ambitions.

**B** It identifies the subject of the first paragraph.

**C** It shows that the writer wants to be taken very seriously.

**D** It makes the reader curious until the end, when it is explained.

# Reading Practice

**Read this selection. Then answer the questions that follow.**

## The City Is So Big
### *by Richard Garcia*

My notes about
what I am reading

The city is so big
Its bridges <u>quake</u> with fear
I know, I have seen at night

The lights sliding from house to house
5 And trains pass with windows shining
Like a smile full of teeth

I have seen machines eating houses
And stairways walk all by themselves
And elevator doors opening and closing
10 And people disappear.

"The City Is So Big" from *Selected Poetry* by Richard Garcia. Text copyright © 1973 by Richard
Garcia. Published by Quinto Sol Publications, Inc. Reprinted by permission of the author.

**GO ON**

---

**Use "The City Is So Big" (p. 60) to answer questions 1–3.**

---

**1** In line 2, the word <u>quake</u> means —

A crack

B cause

C tremble

D watch

**2** Read these lines from the poem.

> *And trains pass with windows shining*
> *Like a smile full of teeth*

In these lines, the poet uses —

F a metaphor to compare watching a train pass to visiting the dentist

G personification to show how a smile can sometimes feel sad

H hyperbole to exaggerate how shiny the train's windows are

J a simile to describe how a train's windows look like a row of teeth

**3** In the last stanza (lines 7–10), what main idea is conveyed through the poet's use of personification, or giving human qualities to a non-human thing?

A The city at night is different from the city during the day.

B Cities are constantly changing.

C Big cities are technologically advanced.

D There can be something frightening and impersonal about a big city.

# Reading Practice

**Read this selection. Then answer the questions that follow.**

## from Yuuki and the Tsunami

*Based on a story retold by Elaine L. Lindy*
*Adapted as a play script by P. J. Rittiger*

My notes about
what I am reading

---

**CHARACTERS**

| | |
|---|---|
| Yuuki | First Villager |
| Yuuki's Father | Second Villager |
| Yuuki's Mother | Other Villagers |
| Village Boy | |

---

**Yuuki:** *(sadly)* Father, tell me again about Grandfather.

**Yuuki's Father:** Everyone in our village remembers your
Grandfather. He was the man who taught us how to
grow rice so well. Everyone respected him because he
5 was so smart. I know that you miss him.

**Yuuki:** Yes, I miss seeing him in our fields each day and
hearing his stories.

*[Yuuki's Mother steps out of the home. She is carrying
a basket of fruit as if she has been cooking inside.*
10 *First Villager, Village Boy, and Other Villagers walk back
and forth across the stage in little groups. They are
decorating the village, so they are carrying baskets,
paper lanterns, bowls of food, and flower garlands.]*

**Yuuki's Mother:** There you two are! Fooling around
15 again! Snap out of it! We have a lot to do before tonight,
you know. If this is going to be a great celebration, then
we better get to work! Am I the only one who knows how
to work around here?

---

**GO ON ➡**

**Yuuki's Father:** Yuuki and I were just talking about
20 Grandfather and what a smart man he was, Mother.

My notes about
what I am reading

**Yuuki's Mother:** Yes, we all miss Grandfather, Yuuki.
Still, we remember him every day by doing things the
way that he taught us.
*(to Yuuki's Father)*
25 OK, that's enough memories for today. Let's get
cracking![1] I need your help inside. Yuuki can work by
himself for a while.

**Yuuki's Father:** Yes, I will come with you, dear.

**Yuuki's Mother:** *(gives basket of fruit to Yuuki)* Yuuki,
30 I want you to take this fruit to the sea and make sure it is
scrubbed clean and dried by the time I return.
*(walks off-stage)*

**Yuuki's Father:** You know how she gets before a
festival. I had better go to help her.
35 *(quickly runs off stage after Yuuki's Mother)*

*[First Villager, Village Boy, and Other Villagers have
been walking back and forth across the stage behind
Yuuki and his family. Now, Yuuki holds the fruit and
walks slowly across the stage. He feels the earth shake
40 under his feet but no one else seems to notice. Yuuki
spins pinwheels with his arms and <u>wobbles</u> his legs so
it looks as if he is trying to stand up on a moving
trampoline.]*

**Yuuki:** *(surprised)* WHAT was THAT? The earth
45 MOVED!

*[The earth moves again. The actors drop what they are
carrying and bend their knees as if trying to keep
balanced. The movement stops and the villagers start to
laugh, relieved.]*

50 **First Villager:** Losing your balance there?

**Second Villager:** No way! I have the sure-footedness of
a mountain!

**First Villager:** What are you talking about? A mountain
has no feet!

1. **Let's get cracking:** let's get busy.

55 **Second Villager:** Haven't you ever heard of the "foot of
the mountain"?

*[First Villager claps Second Villager gently on the
shoulder and the two of them exit, laughing.]*

**Yuuki:** *(seriously)* Wait! The earth MOVED under my
60 feet! I think it WAS an earthquake!

**First Villager:** Come on, Yuuki! Always thinking the
worst.

**Second Villager:** We have not had an earthquake in a
long time. What makes you think we are going to have
65 one now?

**First Villager:** You just don't know how to have fun,
Yuuki. Always working, just like your grandfather.

*[All of the Villagers pick up what they dropped and
start to go about their business again as if nothing has
70 happened.]*

**Yuuki:** *(loudly)* WAIT!
*[Yuuki looks at the back wall of the room. Puts up a
hand to shade his eyes. With the other hand, he points
over the heads of the people in the audience.]* I SEE
75 THE HOUSES BELOW HAVE MOVED! LOOK! THE
SEA HAS TURNED BLACK. NOW IT LOOKS LIKE THE
SEA IS RUNNING BACKWARD, AWAY FROM OUR
VILLAGE!
*(to audience)*
80 Now I remember what Grandfather said! The sea would
turn black and run away from the shore just before . . .
just before . . . a TSUNAMI![2]

*[All Villagers walk to where Yuuki is standing.]*

**First Villager:** LOOK! I have never seen anything like
85 this before! Look how far the ocean has pulled back! We
can see parts of the beach that we never saw before!

**Second Villager:** Yes! Let's go to the beach right away.
Imagine all of the cool shells we will be able to find!
We can string them together and hang them in our trees.
90 We will have the best festival ever!

---

2. **tsunami:** a huge ocean wave caused by an underwater earthquake or
a volcanic eruption.

**GO ON** ➡

[As the Villagers are leaving the stage to run to the
beach, Yuuki waves his arms to try to stop them.]

My notes about
what I am reading

**Yuuki:** WAIT! Wait everyone! Come! Come! There is
terrible danger! My grandfather told me that this is just
95 what happens before a TSUNAMI!!

**Second Villager:** What are you talking about, Yuuki?
Wait . . . are you trying to keep us away so you can get
all the shells for yourself?

**First Villager:** Yuuki! YOU of all people!

100 **Second Villager:** (clicking lips) Tsk, tsk, tsk.

**Yuuki:** No! NO! You don't understand! You must run
away! Up to the mountain! Everybody!

[All the Villagers except the Village Boy leave the stage
laughing to head for the beach. Yuuki yells after them
105 but they do not act like they hear him. Yuuki knows he
has to find a way to get the Villagers to move up to the
mountain quickly. He takes a long piece of wood from
the "fire" in front of his home and runs to the side of the
stage, pretending to set the rice stacks on fire. While he
110 is doing this, Village Boy sits down in front of Yuuki's
house and watches him. Yuuki touches the wood with
the fire on the end to the rice crop in several places.
Then he drops the branch and runs to the front of the
stage facing the audience.]

115 **Yuuki:** FIRE! FIRE! EVERYONE RUN TO THE
MOUNTAIN! QUICK!
(Throws down the burning branch and runs off stage.)


(End of ACT 1)


ACT 2

[All of the characters are standing together on the top of
the mountain, including Yuuki, Yuuki's Mother, and
120 Yuuki's Father, who are standing in front of the other
villagers. Everyone is panting as if they have run a long
way on a hot afternoon. Everyone looks angry and
upset.]

GO ON

**Village Boy:** *(steps forward and points to Yuuki)*
125 YUUKI IS CRAZY! He set fire to the rice crop!
*(to the rest of the Villagers)*
He did it on purpose! I SAW him!

*[Yuuki's Mother and Yuuki's Father step to Yuuki. They are frowning.]*

130 **Yuuki's Mother:** *(crosses arms over her chest)*
I do not believe a word of it. Not my Yuuki. Son, tell them that this is not true!

**Yuuki's Father:** Tell them, Yuuki!

*[Yuuki looks away.]*

135 **Village Boy:** LOOK! LOOK!
*(points over the heads of the people in the audience again)*
A TSUNAMI!

*[All characters on stage gasp, hug each other and hide
140 their faces in their hands in fear, except Yuuki, who stares outward over the heads of the people in the audience as if he is looking at something very far away.]*

**Yuuki:** It was just how Grandfather described a tsunami. Everything he said would happen came true.
145 First comes the earthquake.
*(makes a sweeping motion with the hands away from the body)*
Then, the sea turns black and pulls away from the land.
Then, the tsunami comes and everything is swept away.

150 **Village Boy:** *(sadly)* Our village is gone. The tsunami took it away like it was never there.

**Yuuki:** I am so sorry that I burned the fields. I had to find a way to get everyone to go to the top of the mountain.

**Yuuki's Father:** Yuuki, you saved us all!

My notes about
what I am reading

Name _____ Date _____

---

**Use the excerpt from "Yuuki and the Tsunami" (pp. 62–66) to answer questions 1–7.**

---

**1** What does Yuuki's grandfather represent in the play?

  **A** Old age

  **B** Wisdom

  **C** Superstition

  **D** Happiness

**2** Which line from the play gives you the clearest idea of the character who speaks it?

  **F** *Everyone respected him because he was so smart.*

  **G** *Look how far the ocean has pulled back!*

  **H** *There you two are! Fooling around again! Snap out of it!*

  **J** *We have not had an earthquake in a long time.*

**3** A synonym for <u>wobbles</u> in line 41 is —

  **A** bends

  **B** looks at

  **C** straightens

  **D** shakes

**4** Which lines reveal the play's conflict, or the central problem faced by the main character?

  **F** Lines 14–18

  **G** Lines 36–43

  **H** Lines 93–95

  **J** Lines 143–149

**5** What do the stage directions in line 134 tell you about Yuuki's feelings at this point in the play?

  **A** He feels confident about what he has done.

  **B** He is angry at the villagers for criticizing him.

  **C** He is nervous about telling his parents the truth.

  **D** He feels sad that his grandfather is not there.

**6** Based on Yuuki's actions and dialogue in the play, which statement is accurate?

  **F** He would rather talk than work.

  **G** He wants to be a fisherman rather than a farmer.

  **H** He knows what is right but doesn't have the confidence to do it.

  **J** He possesses his grandfather's leadership qualities.

**GO ON ➡**

**7** Read this diagram of events from the play.

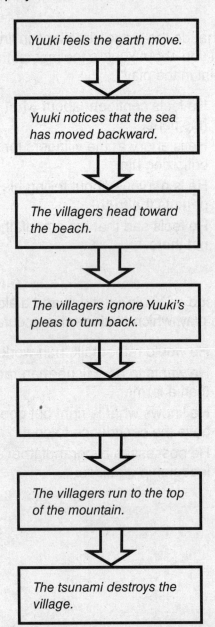

Yuuki feels the earth move.

Yuuki notices that the sea has moved backward.

The villagers head toward the beach.

The villagers ignore Yuuki's pleas to turn back.

The villagers run to the top of the mountain.

The tsunami destroys the village.

Which of the following belongs in the empty box and describes the turning point in the plot?

**A** Yuuki's mother sends him to scrub and dry the fruit for the festival.

**B** The village boy tells what Yuuki has done.

**C** Yuuki sets fire to the rice fields.

**D** The villagers make fun of Yuuki for not wanting them to collect shells.

STOP

Name _____ Date _____

# Reading Practice

**Read this selection. Then answer the questions that follow.**

## from Lies (People Believe) about Animals

*by Susan Sussman and Robert James*

My notes about
what I am reading

### SPIDERS

**Lie:** THE BITE OF A TARANTULA WILL KILL YOU.
**Truth:** NO TARANTULA IS KNOWN TO BE
DANGEROUS TO HUMANS.

1   Years ago, the tarantula's bite was believed to be deadly.
That was before scientists began to study this huge
spider. So far, none of the many species discovered and
studied has proven to be dangerous. What we call a
spider's "poison" is really its *catabolic enzyme,* the same
sort of digestive fluid our bodies use to digest food. Like
that of most spiders, the tarantula's digestive fluid can
kill insects but will leave nothing more serious than an
itchy swelling on a human, if that.

2       It is not possible for a tarantula to walk up and bite
you. Like other spiders, it has no teeth. A spider's
so-called bite is really a pinch made with its two
claw-like legs. The claws poke a couple of holes into
which the spider drips some of that catabolic enzyme.
A tarantula's claws are rarely used in defense, but even
when they are, the tiny pinch is not painful to humans.
The real purpose of the claws is to help the tarantula
catch, hold, and shovel bugs into its mouth.

---

## ALLIGATORS

My notes about what I am reading

**Lie:** ALLIGATORS OFTEN ATTACK PEOPLE.
**Truth:** ALLIGATORS RARELY ATTACK PEOPLE.

3   Alligators know the difference between their natural <u>prey</u> and humans. In Florida, home to nearly a million alligators, records show just five definite and two suspected alligator-caused deaths over the last *thirty years.* If you swim in Florida's fresh waters, there is ninety-five percent probability an alligator is nearby. Obviously, if a million alligators liked the taste of people, there would be many more deaths. "Accidents," the word alligator experts use to describe biting incidents, average five a year. They are called accidents because these bites are provoked attacks caused by people trying to tease or catch alligators or people who feed alligators and hold onto the food too long. Although alligators don't normally attack humans, they *will* defend themselves—either by biting or by lashing out with their mighty tails—when they feel threatened.

## OPOSSUM

**Lie:** THE OPOSSUM SLEEPS HANGING
UPSIDE DOWN BY ITS TAIL.
**Truth:** THE OPOSSUM SLEEPS LYING DOWN.

4   No opossum can sleep hanging by its tail. The tail would relax and unwind. The opossum's tail is *prehensile,* which means it can be used like a fifth hand to grasp items. Although babies are able to hang from their tails, adult opossums are too heavy and would fall. Opossums sleep lying down in earthen dens, under porches, and in other safe havens.

## ELEPHANT

**Lie:** ELEPHANTS DRINK THROUGH THEIR TRUNKS.
**Truth:** ELEPHANTS DRINK THROUGH THEIR
MOUTHS, LIKE ALL ANIMALS.

5   Elephants *seem* to drink through their trunks but are really using them like giant straws to suck up gallons of water. They either squirt the water into their mouths

GO ON ➡

for a drink or spray it over their bodies. The amazing trunk is a six-foot-long nose that the elephant uses for much more than breathing and smelling. It is controlled by forty thousand muscles, and the elephant uses it to pick up the tiniest peanut from the ground or haul huge timbers in the teak forests of Thailand. It can be used as a hand to strip leaves and bark from trees and to pick brush and grass from fields and feed them into the elephant's mouth. The trunk is delicate enough to pat a baby elephant and powerful enough to smash a lion.

6    Elephants are the largest living land mammals in the world. Like all of the large land mammals, they are *herbivores,* or plant-eating animals. They sleep only four to six hours a day since most of their lives must be spent looking for and eating food. It takes a lot of leaves and grass to fill up animals weighing ten to twelve thousand pounds! Each day, an adult elephant eats four to six hundred pounds of vegetation and drinks sixty gallons of water.

## BATS

**Lie:** BATS ARE BLIND. THIS IS WHERE WE GET THE EXPRESSION "BLIND AS A BAT."
**Truth:** BATS AREN'T BLIND. BATS CAN SEE ABOUT AS WELL AS PEOPLE.

7    It was once thought bats were blind because of the jumpy way some of them swoop up, down, and around in the night sky. We now know bats can see in daylight but not at night. The problem is that bats are *nocturnal,* resting during the day and feeding at night. Finding food in the dark can be tricky. Luckily, bats have a special way of using their mouths and ears to "see" in the dark.

8    With mouths open wide, bats shout a special sound as they fly, a sound too high for us humans to hear. (The bat sounds we *can* hear are not food-finding cries, but the much lower-pitched squawks of bats complaining or calling to one another.) When the sound hits something—a moth, a tree, a firefly—it bounces an echo back to the bat. This is called *echolocation.* The bat can tell one echo from another, which is why it will gobble up the moth and firefly but not the tree. If a bat swoops towards you, as bats will do, it's because its

GO ON

sound waves are bouncing off your buttons, barrettes, etc. As soon as the bat realizes those small objects are not bugs, it will swerve away.

My notes about
what I am reading

## BEARS

**Lie:** BEARS HIBERNATE ALL WINTER.
**Truth:** SOME BEARS SLEEP MORE IN WINTER, BUT NONE ARE TRUE HIBERNATORS.

9   True hibernators (like the groundhog) enter a deathlike sleep in which their body temperatures drop, they barely breathe, and their hearts hardly beat. Body functions of most bears slow only slightly in winter. They still get up occasionally and move around, leaving their dens to forage for food. And some bears, like the male polar bear, grizzly bear, and bears in warm climates, may not enter a winter sleep at all.

10   . . . A male bear does not stay with his family. Soon after the male mates with the female, he wanders off. The female bear gives birth in her den around January or February. The inch-and-a-half-long babies are born blind and bald. One of the fastest-growing animal babies in the world, baby bears will weigh ten to fifteen pounds by the time they leave the den in spring. The female must protect her cubs from males, who have been known to eat baby bears.

GO ON

Use the excerpt from *Lies (People Believe) about Animals* (pp. 69–72) to answer questions 1–6.

**1** What purpose do the "Lie" and "Truth" statements serve in the article?

**A** They signal the article's cause-and-effect structure.

**B** They intentionally present misinformation.

**C** They introduce each section of the article.

**D** They summarize the ideas that come before them.

**2** Which statement from the selection proves wrong the common belief that the bite of a tarantula is deadly to humans?

**F** *Years ago, the tarantula's bite was believed to be deadly.*

**G** *[T]he tarantula's digestive fluid can kill insects but will leave nothing more serious than an itchy swelling on a human. . . .*

**H** *It is not possible for a tarantula to walk up and bite you.*

**J** *The real purpose of the claws is to help the tarantula catch, hold, and shovel bugs into its mouth.*

**3** In paragraph 3, the word <u>prey</u> means —

**A** the animals that a meat-eating animal usually hunts and eats

**B** an aggressive or frightening animal that hunts other animals

**C** a part of an animal's natural habitat, including its hunting grounds

**D** to plead for help

**4** Which of the following best summarizes the selection?

**F** People hold many beliefs about animals that are incorrect, including whether they pose danger to humans, how they behave, and what they are able to do.

**G** Spiders don't actually bite, opossums don't actually sleep hanging by their tails, and bears don't really hibernate, even though people think all of these things are true.

**H** People have learned many surprising things about animals over the years.

**J** Everyone misunderstands spiders, alligators, opossums, elephants, bats, and bears.

GO ON

**5** With which of the following statements would the authors most likely agree?

**A** People don't know much about animals.

**B** Animals do not purposely harm humans.

**C** We continue to learn more about animals.

**D** It is impossible to understand why animals behave as they do.

**6** The authors most likely wrote this article to —

**F** persuade readers to stop believing everything they hear

**G** provide information to help readers better understand animals

**H** entertain readers by making fun of the ridiculous ideas some people have

**J** reflect on how they gave up mistaken beliefs based on incorrect information about animals

Name _____ Date _____

# Reading Practice

**Read this selection. Then answer the questions that follow.**

## America Is Stronger When All of Us Take Care of All of Us

*by Christopher Reeve*

My notes about
what I am reading

*Christopher Reeve, an actor famous for his many movie roles,
including that of Superman, was paralyzed in a horseback-
riding accident in 1995. As a result of this life-changing
event, he became an energetic advocate for the disabled
until his death in 2004. He delivered the following speech to
the Democratic National Convention in 1996.*

1    Over the last few years, we've heard a lot about
something called family values. And like many of you
I've struggled to figure out what that means but since
my accident I've found a definition that seems to make
sense. I think it means that we're all family, that we all
have value. And if that's true, if America really is a family,
then we have to recognize that many of our family are
hurting.

2    Just take one aspect of it, one in five of us has some
kind of disability. You may have an aunt with Parkinson's
disease. A neighbor with a spinal cord injury. A brother
with AIDS. And if we're really committed to this idea of
family, we've got to do something about it.

3    First of all, our nation cannot <u>tolerate</u> discrimination
of any kind. That's why the Americans with Disabilities
Act[1] is so important and must be honored everywhere.
It is a civil rights law that is tearing down barriers both
in architecture and in attitude. Its purpose is to give
the disabled access not only to buildings, but to every
opportunity in society. I strongly believe our nation must
give its full support to the caregivers who are helping

---

1. **Americans with Disabilities Act:** passed in 1990 and enacted in 1992 with the
purpose of making services and employment opportunities accessible to Americans
with disabilities.

---

**GO ON** ➡

My notes about
what I am reading

people with disabilities live independent lives. Sure, we've got to balance the budget. And we will. We have to be extremely careful with every dollar that we spend. But we've also got to take care of our family and not slash programs people need. We should be enabling, healing, curing. One of the smartest things we can do about disability is invest in research that will protect us from disease and lead to cures. This country already has a long history of doing just that.

4       When we put our minds to a problem, we can usually find solutions. But our scientists can do more. And we've got to give them the chance. That means more funding for research. Right now, for example, about a quarter-million Americans have a spinal cord injury. Our government spends about $8.7 billion a year just maintaining these members of our family. But we spend only $40 million a year on research that would actually improve the quality of their lives, get them off public assistance, or even cure them. We've got to be smarter, do better. Because the money we invest in research today is going to determine the quality of life of members of our family tomorrow.

5       During my rehabilitation, I met a young man named Gregory Patterson. When he was innocently driving through Newark, New Jersey, a stray bullet from a gang shooting went through his car window, right into his neck and severed his spinal cord. Five years ago, he might have died. Today because of research he's alive. But merely alive is not enough. We have a moral and an economic responsibility to ease his suffering and prevent others from experiencing such pain. And to do that, we don't need to raise taxes. We just need to raise our expectations.

6       America has a tradition many nations probably envy; we frequently achieve the impossible. That's part of our national character. That's what got us from one coast to another. That's what got us the largest economy in the world. That's what got us to the moon. On the wall of my room when I was in rehab was a picture of the space shuttle blasting off, autographed by every astronaut now at NASA. On top of the picture it says, "We found nothing is impossible." That should be our motto. Not

GO ON

a Democratic motto, not a Republican motto. But an American motto. Because this is not something one party can do alone. It's something that we as a nation must do together.

My notes about what I am reading

7    So many of our dreams at first seem impossible, then they seem improbable, and then, when we summon the will, they soon become inevitable. If we can conquer outer space, we should be able to conquer inner space too. The frontier of the brain, the central nervous system, and all the afflictions of the body that destroy so many lives, and rob our country of so much potential. Research can provide hope for people who suffer from Alzheimer's. We've already discovered the gene that causes it.

8    Research can provide hope for people like Muhammad Ali and the Reverend Billy Graham who suffer from Parkinson's. Research can provide hope for millions of Americans like Kirk Douglas, who suffer from stroke. We can ease the pain of people like Barbara Jordan, who battled multiple sclerosis. We can find treatments for people like Elizabeth Glaser, whom we lost to AIDS. Now that we know that nerves in the spinal cord can regenerate, we are on the way to getting millions of people around the world like me up, and out of our wheelchairs.

9    Fifty-six years ago, FDR[2] dedicated new buildings for the National Institute of Health. He said, "the defense this nation seeks, involves a great deal more than building airplanes, ships, guns and bombs. We cannot be a strong nation unless we are a healthy nation." He could have said that today. President Roosevelt showed us that a man who could barely lift himself out of a wheelchair could still lift a nation out of despair. And I believe and so does this Administration in the most important principle FDR taught us: America does not let its needy citizens fend for themselves. America is stronger when all of us take care of all of us. Giving new life to that ideal is the challenge before us tonight. Thank you very much.

2. **FDR:** Franklin Delano Roosevelt was stricken with the crippling disease of polio at age 39. He was largely confined to a wheelchair for the rest of his life. In spite of his disability, he became governor of New York and then president of the United States. He served as president from 1932 until his death in 1945.

Use "America Is Stronger When All of Us Take Care of All of Us" (pp. 75–77) to answer questions 1–7.

**1** Which of the following best expresses the purpose of Reeve's speech?

 **A** To explain the meaning of "family values"

 **B** To urge continued efforts on behalf of disabled Americans

 **C** To describe the achievements of many disabled Americans

 **D** To convince voters to pass the Americans with Disabilities Act

**2** Read the following dictionary entry.

> **tolerate** \tŏl´ə rāt\ v. **1.** to allow or permit **2.** to respect **3.** to endure or suffer through **4.** to be able to undergo a particular medical treatment without negative side effects

What is the definition of <u>tolerate</u> as it is used in paragraph 3?

 **F** Definition 1
 **G** Definition 2
 **H** Definition 3
 **J** Definition 4

**3** In paragraph 6, when Reeve says that achieving the impossible is part of "our national character," he is appealing to listeners' —

 **A** pride
 **B** fear
 **C** pity
 **D** logic

**4** Read this sentence from paragraph 7.

> If we can conquer outer space, we should be able to conquer inner space too.

Why is this an example of faulty reasoning?

 **F** Reeve uses circular reasoning, simply repeating his claim rather than proving it.

 **G** Reeve relies on a testimonial from an unreliable source.

 **H** The statement stereotypes scientists as people who act like conquerors.

 **J** Reeve makes a false comparison between two very different scientific efforts.

**5** Which of the following sentences from the speech provides evidence for Reeve's claim that we should increase funding for medical research?

 **A** And if that's true, if America really is a family, then we have to recognize that many of our family are hurting.

 **B** [The Americans with Disabilities Act] is a civil rights law that is tearing down barriers both in architecture and in attitude.

 **C** Now that we know that nerves in the spinal cord can regenerate, we are on the way to getting millions of people around the world like me up, and out of our wheelchairs.

 **D** President Roosevelt showed us that a man who could barely lift himself out of a wheelchair could still lift a nation out of despair.

GO ON

**6** Examine the cause-effect chart below.

Cause                                    Effects

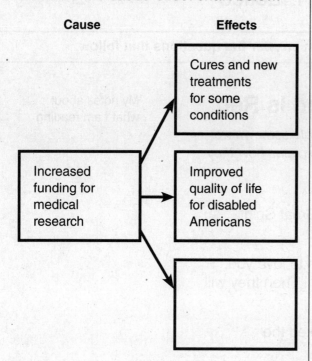

Which of the following does Reeve imply belongs in the empty box?

**F**   Higher taxes

**G**   Ability of more disabled people to live independently without government assistance

**H**   Decreased funding for other government programs, such as space exploration

**J**   Attraction of scientists from other countries

**7** From Reeve's reference to President Roosevelt in the last paragraph of his speech, it is clear that he —

**A**   thinks the president should have done more for other disabled Americans

**B**   believes that America was stronger when led by President Roosevelt

**C**   admires the president for his personal and political accomplishments

**D**   wants the next president to be from the Democratic Party

# Reading Practice

> **Read the next two selections. Then answer the questions that follow.**

## Why the Woodpecker's Head Is Red

My notes about
what I am reading

*Most woodpeckers have patches of red visible somewhere
on their heads. This Native American myth explains how they
came to have this distinctive trait.*

1    One day the woodpecker said to the Great Spirit,
"Men do not like me. I wish they did."

2    The Great Spirit said, "If you wish men to love you,
you must be good to them and help them. Then they will
call you their friend."

3    "How can a little bird help a man?" asked the
woodpecker.

4    "If one wishes to help, the day will come when he can
help," said the Great Spirit. The day did come, and this
story shows how a little bird helped a strong warrior.

5    There was once a cruel magician who lived in a
gloomy wigwam beside the Black-Sea-Water. He did not
like flowers, and they did not blossom in his pathway.
He did not like birds, and they did not sing in the trees
above him. The breath of his nostrils was fatal to all life.
North, south, east, and west he blew the deadly fever
that killed the women and the little children.

6    "Can I help them?" thought a brave warrior, and he
said, "I will find the magician, and see if death will not
come to him as he has made it come to others. I will go
straightway to his home."

7    For many days the brave warrior was in his canoe
traveling across the Black-Sea-Water. At last he saw the
gloomy wigwam of the cruel magician. He shot an arrow
at the door and called, "Come out, O coward! You have
killed women and children with your fatal breath, but you
cannot kill a warrior. Come out and fight, if you are not
afraid."

"Why the Woodpecker's Head is Red" from *The Book of Nature Myths* by Florence Holbrook.
Published by Houghton, Mifflin and Company, 1902.

**GO ON**

8    The cruel magician laughed loud and long. "One breath of fever," he said, "and you will fall to the earth." The warrior shot again, and then the magician was angry. He did not laugh, but he came straight out of his gloomy lodge, and as he came, he blew the fever all about him.

9    Then was seen the greatest fight that the sun had ever looked upon. The brave warrior shot his flint-tipped arrows, but the magician had on his magic cloak, and the arrows could not wound him. He blew from his nostrils the deadly breath of fever, but the heart of the warrior was so strong that the fever could not kill him.

10    At last the brave warrior had but three arrows in his quiver. "What shall I do?" he said sadly. "My arrows are good and my aim is good, but no arrow can go through the magic cloak."

11    "Come on, come on," called the magician. "You are the man who wished to fight. Come on." Then a woodpecker in a tree above the brave warrior said softly, "Aim your arrow at his head, O warrior! Do not shoot at his heart, but at the <u>crest</u> of feathers on his head. He can be wounded there, but not in his heart."

12    The warrior was not so proud that he could not listen to a little bird. The magician bent to lift a stone, and an arrow flew from the warrior's bow. It buzzed and stung like a wasp. It came so close to the crest of feathers that the magician trembled with terror. Before he could run, another arrow came, and this one struck him right on his crest. His heart grew cold with fear. "Death has struck me," he cried.

13    "Your cruel life is over," said the warrior. "People shall no longer fear your fatal breath." Then he said to the woodpecker, "Little bird, you have been a good friend to me, and I will do all that I can for you." He put some of the red blood of the magician upon the little creature's head. It made the crest of feathers there as red as flame. "Whenever a man looks upon you," said the warrior, "he will say, 'That bird is our friend. He helped to kill the cruel magician.'"

My notes about what I am reading

14    The little woodpecker was very proud of his red crest because it showed that he was the friend of man, and all his children to this day are as proud as he was.

My notes about
what I am reading

© George Grall/National Geographic/Getty Images

# Species in an Ecosystem: Niches

My notes about what I am reading

*The myth you just read presents an explanation for the woodpecker's red coloring. This expository selection describes how an organism, a specific kind of animal, relates to its surroundings. These surroundings—the organism's ecosystem—include two kinds of factors: biotic factors, which are other living things; and abiotic factors, which are nonliving elements such as temperature, wind, and soil.*

1    Each organism in an ecosystem has its own niche or role in that ecosystem. A species' niche is its relationship with the biotic and abiotic factors of the ecosystem. It includes where it lives, and how it raises its young.

2    Part of an animal's niche is defined by what it eats and what eats it. A predator is an animal, such as a lynx,[1] that eats other animals, such as hares.[2] The animal that is eaten—the hare—is the prey. Both predators and prey are <u>adapted</u> for their niches. A lynx, for example, can run fast and can easily see and smell prey. Hares also run fast, and their fur usually blends into the background.

3    Some species are generalists, meaning they occupy a broad niche. For example, raccoons are predators that eat almost anything. They dine on nuts, berries, birds, fish, and even garbage!

4    Other species are specialists, meaning they occupy a very specific niche. Evergreen forests are home to five species of insect-eating wood warblers.[3] All five types hunt in the same trees in the forest. But each warbler species works in a different part of the trees. Two species hunt in different parts of the top section of the trees. Two other species hunt in different parts of the middle section. One species spends most of its time hunting in the bottom section of the trees.

---

1. **lynx:** a kind of wildcat with a short tail and tufted ears.
2. **hare:** an animal similar to a rabbit but with longer ears and legs.
3. **warbler:** a small songbird.

---

Excerpt from *Houghton Mifflin Science*, Student Edition, Level 6 by Valentino, et al. Copyright © 2007 by Houghton Mifflin Company. All rights reserved. Reprinted by permission of Houghton Mifflin Harcourt Publishing Company.

GO ON

My notes about
what I am reading

5    The warblers' niches are different in another way.
     They nest and raise their young at different times.
     Because they need more food while they are raising
     young, nesting at different times means that all species
     do not need more food at the same time.

6    The five species of warblers can all survive in the
     same trees because their niches are different. When
     two species have exactly the same niche, they compete
     for the same resources. Over time, one species is more
     successful and the other species cannot survive in the
     ecosystem.

**Use "Why the Woodpecker's Head Is Red" (pp. 80–82) to answer questions 1–6.**

**1** Which of these is the best plot summary of the myth?

**A** There is a cruel magician who brings trouble and death to all in the land. A warrior sets out to kill him. After a fierce battle, he succeeds.

**B** A woodpecker wants people to like him. The Great Spirit tells him to be patient and he will get the chance to help a person. Eventually, the woodpecker is able to help a human being.

**C** A woodpecker helps a warrior defeat a cruel magician by telling him to aim for the magician's head. In gratitude, the warrior places some of the magician's blood on the bird's head to show the world that he is a friend to humans.

**D** It is unclear why woodpeckers have red on their heads. One story is that they helped a warrior kill an evil magician. The magician had a crest of feathers on his head. We may never know the real reason that woodpeckers have red heads.

**2** Which words from paragraph 11 help you figure out the meaning of crest?

**F** *shoot at his heart*

**G** *in a tree above*

**H** *feathers on his head*

**J** *the brave warrior*

**3** Which of the following best expresses the theme of this tale, or its message about life?

**A** Cruelty has always existed in one form or another.

**B** The red on woodpeckers' heads distinguishes them from other birds.

**C** Those who take the opportunity to help others are often rewarded.

**D** In ancient times, people had many unanswered questions about nature.

**4** Which common feature of traditional literature contributes to the conflict in this story?

**F** Hyperbole, or exaggeration, to make a hero seem larger than life

**G** The use of magic

**H** Powerful beings in disguise

**J** The rule of three

GO ON

**5** Read this line from the myth: "Then was seen the greatest fight that the sun had ever looked upon." This is an example of —

**A** simile

**B** refrain

**C** understatement

**D** personification

**6** Think about the photograph on page 82 and how it relates to the story. Which of the following would be the best caption for the photograph?

**F** Woodpeckers like this one feed on insects and sap beneath the bark of trees.

**G** Woodpeckers are known for making a lot of noise when they make holes in trees.

**H** This woodpecker has a crest of feathers like the one the warrior turned red with the magician's blood.

**J** You can see from this photo that the woodpecker is a great friend of humans.

GO ON ➡

Name _____ Date _____

**7** A synonym for the word <u>adapted</u> in paragraph 2 is —

**A** suited
**B** hungry
**C** unfit
**D** identified

**8** Which inference or conclusion is supported by the facts in paragraphs 3 and 4?

**F** Small animals, such as birds, have more specialized diets than large animals.
**G** Generalists would find it easier to survive than specialists if their environment changed.
**H** Warblers are uncommon birds.
**J** Raccoons prefer to live in urban neighborhoods.

**9** Each animal has its own niche because —

**A** every species of animal is different
**B** an ecosystem's resources are limited
**C** some organisms have more offspring than others
**D** they help scientists identify species of organisms

GO ON

**10** Which of the following best describes the overall organization of the selection?

**F** The writer compares and contrasts the diets and behaviors of various organisms in an ecosystem.

**G** The writer explains what a niche is and provides specific examples of animals and their niches.

**H** The writer traces the development of niches within an ecosystem.

**J** The writer classifies the kinds of animals that belong to various niches.

**11** Which is the best summary of the selection?

**A** Each species in an ecosystem occupies its own niche, which is defined by what it eats and where it lives. Niches allow many different kinds of organisms to thrive in the same environment.

**B** Warblers are unique birds that live in the same kind of tree but eat different insects from different parts of the tree. They also raise their young at different times.

**C** Some animals are limited in what they eat. They may hunt a specific type of prey. Others have more flexibility.

**D** Nature has an amazing organization that humans are not always aware of. The fact that each species has its own niche illustrates this fact.

**GO ON**

Use "Why the Woodpecker's Head Is Red" and "Species in an Ecosystem: Niches"
(pp. 80–84) to answer questions 12–13.

**12** The details in both the myth and the expository selection support the inference that —

**F** many species are in danger of becoming extinct

**G** the relationship between humans and nature is complex

**H** as human knowledge increases, people are better able to explain occurrences in nature

**J** there is no scientific reason for why some species survive and others do not

**13** Which statement about the two selections is accurate?

**A** The two selections have a different approach to their subject but a similar purpose.

**B** The content of both selections is based on fact.

**C** Both selections explain how animals choose where they live.

**D** The tone of both selections is objective.

# Written Composition

# Written Composition: Personal Narrative 1

## READ

Sometimes we learn new skills easily. Other times it seems as if we will never learn how to do something. We might give up, decide to try harder, or even ask for help.

## THINK

Think about a time when you had trouble learning a new skill. Did you feel like giving up? What made you keep trying? How did you feel when you finally succeeded?

## WRITE

Write a personal narrative telling about a time when you had to work hard to learn a new skill.

**As you write your composition, remember to —**

☐ focus on a controlling idea about a time when you struggled to learn a new skill

☐ organize events in a way that makes sense, such as chronological (time) order; connect ideas using transitions

☐ develop your ideas fully and thoughtfully, including the reasons for your actions

☐ make sure your composition is no longer than one page

**TEKS 14A, 14B, 14C, 14D, 16, 19, 20, 21**

**ANALYZE THE PROMPT**
The prompt asks you to write a personal narrative. That means you should write about your own experience. You should not write a made-up story or tell about something that happened to someone else.

**RESPOND TO THE PROMPT**

- **Plan** by listing skills that you have. Circle those that were hard to learn. Choose the one that you most clearly remember learning. Jot down details about that experience and put them in order.
- **Draft** your response by describing the key events of your experience in sequence. Identify the skill, why it was challenging, and how you mastered it.
- **Revise** to use more precise wording, to vary your sentences, and to add transitions.
- **Edit** your writing to correct any errors in spelling, grammar, punctuation, or capitalization.

Name _____ Date _____

# Benchmark Composition: Personal Narrative 1 **Score Point 4**

## I Can Juggle!

One cold, rainy Saturday afternoon, after hearing me complain about having nothing to do, my mother drove me to the local bookstore. I wandered through the "how-to-do" section, but nothing seemed interesting. Then, a little yellow book caught my eye. It was entitled <u>Learn to Juggle</u>. Okay! Maybe I would!

After reading the book, I decided that juggling would be easy. After all, it was just a pattern of throwing and catching balls. I eagerly tore open the package of balls that came with the book and began to practice. Unfortunately, juggling wasn't as simple as I had thought. I couldn't even perform three throws and catches. Angry, I threw balls on the floor and went to bed.

The next morning, after eating breakfast, I walked into my room to find the book staring menacingly at me. It seemed to be challenging me to try juggling again. I accepted the challenge and started where I left off the day before. And, juggling was a little easier. Practicing for what seemed like hours, I was amazed to find that I could perform up to five throws and catches.

I practiced for five more days in a row, getting my number up to 15 throws and catches. But compared to professionals, my juggling was choppy and awkward. I had to think about which hand I needed to throw or catch with. After six more days of practicing with no visible results, I gave up. So what if I didn't learn to juggle? It wasn't as if my life depended on it.

But, as the days passed, I found myself drawn back to my juggling. Finally, after a week of avoiding it, I picked up the balls and started. From the first toss, I knew something was different. My arms were coordinated and fluid, barely moving with each throw. My hands were as light as feathers, catching every ball with ease. I began counting and was soon up to 50. I stood in the middle of my room, in awe of what I had just done.

I could not hold in my emotions. Nearly crying, I ran through the entire house showing my family my new skill. There were many thoughts dancing in my head, but one overpowered the others. I was now officially a juggler!

**DEVELOPMENT OF IDEAS**
In the first paragraph, the writer provides details that explain what led to her decision to learn to juggle. She states her controlling idea in the second paragraph.

**DEVELOPMENT OF IDEAS**
In the third paragraph, the writer uses the literary device of personification to help explain her reason for persevering with juggling.

**ORGANIZATION/ PROGRESSION**
Phrases such as "five more days in a row" help to emphasize the amount of effort it took for the writer to learn the skill. These phrases also help readers understand the sequence of events.

**DEVELOPMENT OF IDEAS**
The writer uses detailed description and a simile ("My hands were as light as feathers") to describe finally mastering the skill.

**Personal Narrative 1: Score Summary and Rubric**                    **Score Point 4**

This personal narrative effectively responds to the prompt, clearly showing the writer's struggle to master a new skill. Details show the difficulty of the task as well as the writer's determination and persistence. Literary devices, varied sentence structure, and a strong command of conventions make the writing effective.

| | ORGANIZATION/ PROGRESSION | DEVELOPMENT OF IDEAS | USE OF LANGUAGE CONVENTIONS |
|---|---|---|---|
| 4 | • Uses appropriate structure or form for purpose and demands of prompt; narrative strategies enhance effectiveness of writing<br>• Uses details effectively; sustains focus, creating unity and coherence<br>• Controls progression with transitions showing relationships among ideas | • Employs specific, well-chosen details that develop key literary elements<br>• Engages reader through a thoughtful narrative that may approach topic from an unusual perspective; demonstrates a deep understanding of prompt | • Shows strong understanding of word choice appropriate to form, purpose, and tone<br>• Uses purposeful, varied, and controlled sentences<br>• Demonstrates command of conventions so that narrative is fluent and clear even if the writing contains minor errors |
| 3 | • Uses mostly effective structure or form for demands of prompt; narrative strategies generally enhance effectiveness of writing<br>• Mostly uses details effectively; narrative is coherent though may lack overall unity<br>• Mostly controls progression of ideas with transitions | • Employs specific details that add some substance to the narrative; details generally contribute to key literary elements<br>• Demonstrates some depth of thought, with an original rather than formulaic approach and a good understanding of the task | • Shows a basic understanding of word choice appropriate to form, purpose, and tone; diction generally succeeds in communicating meaning<br>• Uses varied and mostly controlled sentences<br>• Demonstrates general command of conventions; errors do not seriously affect clarity or fluency of narrative |
| 2 | • May use form or structure inappropriate to demands of the prompt; narrative strategies contribute only marginally to effectiveness<br>• May use some details that do not contribute to narrative; focus may not be sustained<br>• Controls progression of thought inconsistently; may lack clear links among ideas | • Fails to develop narrative beyond a minimal level because details may be inappropriate or incompletely developed; details only marginally contribute to key literary elements<br>• Uses somewhat formulaic approach to prompt, reflecting limited understanding of task | • Shows limited understanding of word choice; may use basic or simplistic vocabulary<br>• May use awkward, uncontrolled sentences<br>• Demonstrates partial command of conventions, possibly with significant errors that weaken the fluency of writing |
| 1 | • Uses inappropriate form or structure<br>• Lacks focus and apt details; coherence/unity are weak<br>• Has weak progression of thought, with lack of meaningful transitions | • Exhibits weak development of ideas because details are inappropriate, vague, or insufficient<br>• Demonstrates lack of understanding of prompt and/ or vague approach | • Lacks appropriate word choice; uses imprecise or general vocabulary<br>• Uses simplistic, awkward, or uncontrolled sentences<br>• Demonstrates limited or no command of conventions |

# Benchmark Composition: Personal Narrative 1   Score Point 2

## Free Throw

As a first time basketball player I had not learned how to do one important thing that all basketball players needed and that is a good free throw. On the night before the first game I was very nervous. I still had not figured out how to shoot a free throw. I worried because I couldn't shoot free throws, I thought, I know the perfect person who could help me with this problem, I said, Julian. The next day my attitude had changed significantly because I knew Julian who was the best shooter on the team could help me. When I got to the gym I asked him if he would help me. Coach opened the door, the team got ready. Me and Julian were the first ones on the court for the shoot around so he could help me. The lesson started out with me showing Julian how I shot. He told me to freeze so I could correct my poor form. When Julian was done adjusting my form he told me to shoot. I was nervous but I bent my legs and shot. I did what he told me to and made my free throw. I did it, I learned how to shoot free throws. Learning to shoot these free throws was stressful but all worthwhile in the end. Learning is probably the best part of life.

**DEVELOPMENT OF IDEAS**
The writer clearly identifies the skill and his reason for wanting to learn it. However, the narrative provides few details about his struggle and eventual success.

**USE OF LANGUAGE CONVENTIONS**
This narrative includes several run-on sentences and other grammatical errors, such as the incorrect use of pronouns.

Name _____ Date _____

This personal narrative shows a good understanding of the prompt but is not well developed. The writer repeats some ideas over and over (*I was worried because I couldn't shoot free throws; Julian ... could help me*) but sums up the accomplishment in two sentences (*I ... made my free throw. I did it ...*). Run-on sentences and other errors make the essay less effective.

|   | ORGANIZATION/ PROGRESSION | DEVELOPMENT OF IDEAS | USE OF LANGUAGE CONVENTIONS |
|---|---|---|---|
| 4 | • Uses appropriate structure or form for purpose and demands of prompt; narrative strategies enhance effectiveness of writing <br> • Uses details effectively; sustains focus, creating unity and coherence <br> • Controls progression with transitions showing relationships among ideas | • Employs specific, well-chosen details that develop key literary elements <br> • Engages reader through a thoughtful narrative that may approach topic from an unusual perspective; demonstrates a deep understanding of prompt | • Shows strong understanding of word choice appropriate to form, purpose, and tone <br> • Uses purposeful, varied, and controlled sentences <br> • Demonstrates command of conventions so that narrative is fluent and clear even if the writing contains minor errors |
| 3 | • Uses mostly effective structure or form for demands of prompt; narrative strategies generally enhance effectiveness of writing <br> • Mostly uses details effectively; narrative is coherent though may lack overall unity <br> • Mostly controls progression of ideas with transitions | • Employs specific details that add some substance to the narrative; details generally contribute to key literary elements <br> • Demonstrates some depth of thought, with an original rather than formulaic approach and a good understanding of the task | • Shows a basic understanding of word choice appropriate to form, purpose, and tone; diction generally succeeds in communicating meaning <br> • Uses varied and mostly controlled sentences <br> • Demonstrates general command of conventions; errors do not seriously affect clarity or fluency of narrative |
| 2 | • May use form or structure inappropriate to demands of the prompt; narrative strategies contribute only marginally to effectiveness <br> • May use some details that do not contribute to narrative; focus may not be sustained <br> • Controls progression of thought inconsistently; may lack clear links among ideas | • Fails to develop narrative beyond a minimal level because details may be inappropriate or incompletely developed; details only marginally contribute to key literary elements <br> • Uses somewhat formulaic approach to prompt, reflecting limited understanding of task | • Shows limited understanding of word choice; may use basic or simplistic vocabulary <br> • May use awkward, uncontrolled sentences <br> • Demonstrates partial command of conventions, possibly with significant errors that weaken the fluency of writing |
| 1 | • Uses inappropriate form or structure <br> • Lacks focus and apt details; coherence/unity are weak <br> • Has weak progression of thought, with lack of meaningful transitions | • Exhibits weak development of ideas because details are inappropriate, vague, or insufficient <br> • Demonstrates lack of understanding of prompt and/ or vague approach | • Lacks appropriate word choice; uses imprecise or general vocabulary <br> • Uses simplistic, awkward, or uncontrolled sentences <br> • Demonstrates limited or no command of conventions |

# Written Composition: Personal Narrative 2

**READ**

One of the greatest gifts we can give to others is our support and encouragement when they need it most.

**THINK**

Think about a time in your life when you helped someone out, either by giving advice or encouragement or by taking action. What did you do or say to help? How did your actions or words affect the person? How did you feel knowing you had helped?

**WRITE**

Write a personal narrative about a time when you helped someone else through your words or actions.

**As you write your composition, remember to —**

☐ focus on a controlling idea about a time when you helped or encouraged another person

☐ organize events in an order that makes sense, such as chronological (time) order; connect ideas using transitions

☐ develop your ideas fully and thoughtfully, including the reasons for your actions and the effect they had

☐ make sure your composition is no longer than one page

**TEKS 14A, 14B, 14C, 14D, 16, 19, 20, 21**

**ANALYZE THE PROMPT**
The prompt asks you to write a personal narrative. That means you should write from the first-person point of view, using pronouns like *I* and *we* to describe an experience from your own life.

**RESPOND TO THE PROMPT**
- **Plan** by jotting down all of the times that you can remember helping someone by giving advice, taking action, or just listening. Choose the situation that you can most clearly describe. Identify the situation and what you did.
- **Draft** your response by describing events in the order they happened. Include background details to explain why the person needed help.
- **Revise** to use more precise wording, to vary the lengths and types of sentences you use, and to add transitions.
- **Edit** your writing to correct any errors in spelling, grammar, punctuation, or capitalization.

# Benchmark Composition: Personal Narrative 2    Score Point 4

## You Were There

The other day I was cleaning out my desk and found an e-mail from my friend Pete. He had moved to Minnesota at the end of fifth grade. For some reason, I had printed it out and saved it. Before throwing it out, I decided I had better reread it.

"Dear Steve," I read, "do you remember when we were about 8 years old and you taught me everything there was to know about baseball? I do and always will. We had just moved here and I didn't know anyone. I wandered down to the ball park and was standing on the edge of the field just watching. All of a sudden, I heard a yell. You were waving at me. I panicked and thought I must be in your way, but it turned out that you wanted me to come over and play in the outfield. You told me exactly what to do and how to do it. You backed me up when the fly balls came, and pretty soon, I was really enjoying myself. When it came time for me to bat, you showed me how to stand and swing. You laughed when I told you how nervous I was. Then, you said something I will never forget: 'Don't worry. I've got your back, buddy.' As I think about that day, I realize that you taught me about more than baseball. You really taught me about friendship. I am starting all over again now in Minnesota, but I have a feeling that both lessons will help me. I just wanted to say thanks. You were there when I needed someone. You are a good friend."

I refolded the e-mail and placed it carefully back in my desk drawer. I remembered that day vividly. One of the players for our team hadn't shown up. But there was this skinny kid just hanging around looking lost. It surprised me that he didn't know how to play baseball, but it was a lot of fun teaching him. We hit it off right away and became really good friends. I never dreamed that calling him over would affect his life so much. Reading his e-mail made me proud that I had helped him. It also made me think about how what we do can have consequences that we don't even realize.

Right then, I decided to send Pete an e-mail and suggest that we start making plans to visit each other very soon.

**DEVELOPMENT OF IDEAS**

The opening lines of the essay indicate that the writer is going to take an unusual approach to the prompt. By quoting from Pete's e-mail, he will include someone else's view of events as well as his own.

**DEVELOPMENT OF IDEAS**

The controlling idea is developed throughout the second paragraph with specific details showing what the writer did for his friend. Near the end of the paragraph, the writer states this idea directly.

**ORGANIZATION/ PROGRESSION**

The writer skillfully makes the transition from reading the e-mail back to his own thoughts in the third paragraph.

**DEVELOPMENT OF IDEAS**

The last two paragraphs portray the incident from the writer's point of view. His reflections tell why the event was important.

**Personal Narrative 2: Score Summary and Rubric**                    **Score Point 4**

This writer's approach is effective. His actions are clearly described through the e-mail, and the important ideas are reinforced by his own words in the last paragraphs. The essay engages readers, who can visualize themselves in similar situations. The writer's skillful use of conventions strengthens the content.

| | ORGANIZATION/ PROGRESSION | DEVELOPMENT OF IDEAS | USE OF LANGUAGE CONVENTIONS |
|---|---|---|---|
| 4 | • Uses appropriate structure or form for purpose and demands of prompt; narrative strategies enhance effectiveness of writing<br>• Uses details effectively; sustains focus, creating unity and coherence<br>• Controls progression with transitions showing relationships among ideas | • Employs specific, well-chosen details that develop key literary elements<br>• Engages reader through a thoughtful narrative that may approach topic from an unusual perspective; demonstrates a deep understanding of prompt | • Shows strong understanding of word choice appropriate to form, purpose, and tone<br>• Uses purposeful, varied, and controlled sentences<br>• Demonstrates command of conventions so that narrative is fluent and clear even if the writing contains minor errors |
| 3 | • Uses mostly effective structure or form for demands of prompt; narrative strategies generally enhance effectiveness of writing<br>• Mostly uses details effectively; narrative is coherent though may lack overall unity<br>• Mostly controls progression of ideas with transitions | • Employs specific details that add some substance to the narrative; details generally contribute to key literary elements<br>• Demonstrates some depth of thought, with an original rather than formulaic approach and a good understanding of the task | • Shows a basic understanding of word choice appropriate to form, purpose, and tone; diction generally succeeds in communicating meaning<br>• Uses varied and mostly controlled sentences<br>• Demonstrates general command of conventions; errors do not seriously affect clarity or fluency of narrative |
| 2 | • May use form or structure inappropriate to demands of the prompt; narrative strategies contribute only marginally to effectiveness<br>• May use some details that do not contribute to narrative; focus may not be sustained<br>• Controls progression of thought inconsistently; may lack clear links among ideas | • Fails to develop narrative beyond a minimal level because details may be inappropriate or incompletely developed; details only marginally contribute to key literary elements<br>• Uses somewhat formulaic approach to prompt, reflecting limited understanding of task | • Shows limited understanding of word choice; may use basic or simplistic vocabulary<br>• May use awkward, uncontrolled sentences<br>• Demonstrates partial command of conventions, possibly with significant errors that weaken the fluency of writing |
| 1 | • Uses inappropriate form or structure<br>• Lacks focus and apt details; coherence/unity are weak<br>• Has weak progression of thought, with lack of meaningful transitions | • Exhibits weak development of ideas because details are inappropriate, vague, or insufficient<br>• Demonstrates lack of understanding of prompt and/ or vague approach | • Lacks appropriate word choice; uses imprecise or general vocabulary<br>• Uses simplistic, awkward, or uncontrolled sentences<br>• Demonstrates limited or no command of conventions |

# Benchmark Composition: Personal Narrative 2  Score Point 2

## The Hug

My younger sister was sick a lot last year. Some days her legs hurt so much that she couldn't get out of bed. The doctors gave her medicine. All it did most of the time was make her sleepy. Every day when I came home from school I would go straight to her room or the couch wherever she was. I would give her a big hug I told her about what happened that day. I asked her about her day. I told her the hugs were to take away her pain and ugly thoughts of feeling sorry for herself. One day I could tell she was miserable. I hugged her for a long time and then fell to the ground. I layed there without moving. My sister yelled for my mom, she came running. They were getting scared when I opened my eyes. I looked at my sister and told her that she must have had a lot of ugly thoughts that day, they took all of my energy away! My sister laughed and laughed. She always told me that it meant a lot to her, what I did to make her feel better.

**DEVELOPMENT OF IDEAS**
The details all relate to the controlling idea. However, the key ideas, such as the importance of not feeling sorry for yourself, are poorly developed and leave the reader confused.

**USE OF LANGUAGE CONVENTIONS**
Run-on sentences are distracting and cause the essay to sound less organized than it is.

**Personal Narrative 2: Score Summary and Rubric**    **Score Point 2**

All the details in this personal narrative are relevant. However, there is little concrete description in the writing, making the response less than effective. Although the writer has a fairly good grasp of spelling, the number of run-on sentences is distracting.

| | ORGANIZATION/ PROGRESSION | DEVELOPMENT OF IDEAS | USE OF LANGUAGE CONVENTIONS |
|---|---|---|---|
| **4** | • Uses appropriate structure or form for purpose and demands of prompt; narrative strategies enhance effectiveness of writing<br>• Uses details effectively; sustains focus, creating unity and coherence<br>• Controls progression with transitions showing relationships among ideas | • Employs specific, well-chosen details that develop key literary elements<br>• Engages reader through a thoughtful narrative that may approach topic from an unusual perspective; demonstrates a deep understanding of prompt | • Shows strong understanding of word choice appropriate to form, purpose, and tone<br>• Uses purposeful, varied, and controlled sentences<br>• Demonstrates command of conventions so that narrative is fluent and clear even if the writing contains minor errors |
| **3** | • Uses mostly effective structure or form for demands of prompt; narrative strategies generally enhance effectiveness of writing<br>• Mostly uses details effectively; narrative is coherent though may lack overall unity<br>• Mostly controls progression of ideas with transitions | • Employs specific details that add some substance to the narrative; details generally contribute to key literary elements<br>• Demonstrates some depth of thought, with an original rather than formulaic approach and a good understanding of the task | • Shows a basic understanding of word choice appropriate to form, purpose, and tone; diction generally succeeds in communicating meaning<br>• Uses varied and mostly controlled sentences<br>• Demonstrates general command of conventions; errors do not seriously affect clarity or fluency of narrative |
| **2** | • May use form or structure inappropriate to demands of the prompt; narrative strategies contribute only marginally to effectiveness<br>• May use some details that do not contribute to narrative; focus may not be sustained<br>• Controls progression of thought inconsistently; may lack clear links among ideas | • Fails to develop narrative beyond a minimal level because details may be inappropriate or incompletely developed; details only marginally contribute to key literary elements<br>• Uses somewhat formulaic approach to prompt, reflecting limited understanding of task | • Shows limited understanding of word choice; may use basic or simplistic vocabulary<br>• May use awkward, uncontrolled sentences<br>• Demonstrates partial command of conventions, possibly with significant errors that weaken the fluency of writing |
| **1** | • Uses inappropriate form or structure<br>• Lacks focus and apt details; coherence/unity are weak<br>• Has weak progression of thought, with lack of meaningful transitions | • Exhibits weak development of ideas because details are inappropriate, vague, or insufficient<br>• Demonstrates lack of understanding of prompt and/or vague approach | • Lacks appropriate word choice; uses imprecise or general vocabulary<br>• Uses simplistic, awkward, or uncontrolled sentences<br>• Demonstrates limited or no command of conventions |

# Written Composition: Expository Essay 1

## READ

Throughout your school year, you take quizzes and important tests. Some of these require only a little bit of preparation; others demand that you study hard in order to be ready.

## THINK

Think about how you prepare to take a test in school. What steps do you follow to make sure that you are ready to do your best? How would you explain your process to someone else?

## WRITE

Write an expository essay that explains how to study for a test.

**As you write your composition, remember to —**

☐ focus on a controlling idea that explains how you study for a test

☐ organize your response so that each step of the process is described clearly and in order, using transitions such as *first, next,* and *finally*

☐ develop your ideas fully and thoughtfully, including appropriate facts and details to make the process clear for your readers

☐ make sure your composition is no longer than one page

**TEKS 14A, 14B, 14C, 14D, 17A, 19, 20, 21**

### ANALYZE THE PROMPT
The prompt asks you to explain a procedure for studying for a test. You should not write a story, a description, or a defense of your opinion. Rather, you should provide instructions that explain the steps necessary to prepare for a test.

### RESPOND TO THE PROMPT
- **Plan** by listing all of the steps that you take or know you should take to study for a test. Jot down details that explain each step. Choose the key steps and put them in the correct order.
- **Draft** your response by writing an introduction that states your controlling idea about the best way to prepare for tests. Explain each step fully with examples and details.
- **Revise** to use more precise wording, to vary your sentence types, and to add transitions.
- **Edit** your essay to correct any remaining errors in spelling, grammar, punctuation, and capitalization.

# Benchmark Composition: Expository Essay 1

**Score Point 4**

## Testing, One, Two, Three!

I used to get very nervous about tests. No matter how long I studied, I never did as well as I thought I should. But now I have a new and improved study system. I follow three simple steps every time I need to prepare for a test. Since I started using this system, my grades have gone up. Must be it works!

First, a few days before the test is scheduled, I ask the teacher what the test will cover. Then I make sure I have all the notes, textbook pages, and other assignments related to the topics. I look them over quickly to get an idea of how much material I need to learn or review. This helps me figure out how much time I will need to set aside to study. I also make sure I understand everything. If I don't, I stop in to see the teacher seventh period for extra help.

Next, I prepare my study outline. This might sound complicated, but it really isn't. Two days before the test, I jot down the major topics and important details from the chapter or section to be tested. Sometimes I do a written outline; other times, I create my outline on the computer. This usually takes me about half an hour. Then I use fifteen minutes more to read through my outline and add other details from my notes or textbook. The benefit of this method is that I am studying while I am preparing my study aid. Another big advantage is that for a unit test or final exam, I have all of my study outlines to help me get ready.

Finally, the night before the test, I put the finishing touches on my knowledge! I read through my study outline and highlight ideas that I want to make sure I remember. Sometimes I read my outline aloud to help me focus better. Or, I might ask my mother or sister to listen to me summarize the important information. I spend about fifteen minutes on this step. Then I make sure I relax and get a good night's sleep.

I used to spend hours staring at my books or notes or the computer screen and not remember anything. This system works for me and saves me a lot of time as well. I hope it works for you, too!

**DEVELOPMENT OF IDEAS**
The controlling idea of the essay is established in the first paragraph. The writer's enthusiastic tone engages readers and makes them want to find out more.

**ORGANIZATION/ PROGRESSION**
By using transitions such as *first, next,* and *finally,* the writer makes it easy for readers to identify and follow each step of the process.

**DEVELOPMENT OF IDEAS**
The writer includes specific and precise details that fully explain each step of the study system so that readers can actually use it if they choose.

**ORGANIZATION/ PROGRESSION**
The writer includes phrases such as "a few days before the test," "two days before the test," and "the night before the test" to provide a timeline for readers.

Name _____ Date _____

This expository essay provides a complete "how-to" guide for preparing to take a test. The writer has included detailed explanations of each step and has presented the information in a logical order. Additionally, the writer's style is fluent and shows skillful command of the conventions.

| | ORGANIZATION/ PROGRESSION | DEVELOPMENT OF IDEAS | USE OF LANGUAGE CONVENTIONS |
|---|---|---|---|
| 4 | • Uses appropriate structure for purpose and demands of the prompt<br>• Establishes and sustains focus, unity, and coherence via the controlling idea<br>• Controls progression with transitions showing relationships among ideas | • Employs specific and well-chosen details and examples<br>• Engages the reader through thoughtful development of ideas; may approach topic from an unusual perspective; demonstrates a deep understanding of prompt | • Shows understanding of word choice appropriate to purpose and intended tone<br>• Uses purposeful, varied, and controlled sentences<br>• Demonstrates a command of conventions so that essay is clear and effective even if it contains minor errors |
| 3 | • Uses mostly effective structure for purpose and demands of prompt<br>• Relates most ideas to controlling idea; essay is coherent though may lack overall unity<br>• Mostly controls progression of ideas with transitions | • Employs specific, appropriate details and examples that add some substance to essay<br>• Demonstrates some depth of thought, with an original rather than formulaic approach and a good understanding of the task | • Shows a basic understanding of word choice appropriate to purpose and intended tone<br>• Uses varied and generally controlled sentences<br>• Demonstrates general command of conventions; errors do not seriously affect clarity or fluency |
| 2 | • May use structure that is inappropriate to prompt; structure may not contribute to clarity of explanation<br>• May use weak or unclear controlling idea, reducing focus and coherence<br>• Has inconsistent progression of thought, with too few meaningful transitions and connections | • Lacks strong development of ideas because details are inappropriate or insufficiently developed<br>• Demonstrates little depth of thought, with a formulaic approach to the prompt and a limited understanding of the task | • Shows limited grasp of word choice, failing to establish appropriate tone<br>• Uses awkward or uncontrolled sentences, weakening essay's effectiveness<br>• Demonstrates partial command of conventions; errors may result in a lack of fluency or clarity |
| 1 | • Uses inappropriate or no obvious structure<br>• Lacks clear controlling idea, with resulting weak focus and coherence<br>• Has weak progression of thought, with lack of meaningful transitions and connections among ideas | • Lacks strong development of ideas because details and examples are inappropriate, vague, or insufficient<br>• Demonstrates lack of understanding of prompt through an overall insubstantial essay and/or a vague or confused approach | • Lacks understanding of word choice; vocabulary is imprecise or unsuitable<br>• Uses simplistic, awkward, or uncontrolled sentences, weakening essay's effectiveness<br>• Demonstrates limited or no command of conventions, resulting in a lack of fluency |

# Benchmark Composition: Expository Essay 1

## Feed Your Brain

You know how they say feed a cold starve a fever. I say feed your brain to get ready for a test. This is my study plan. My first step is to get my favorite snacks and something to drink. My second step is to go to my desk and spread out my books and notes. My third step is to read them over. Sometimes out loud. My fourth step is to get my mom to quiz me. For every question I get right. I get to eat a snack. For every question I get wrong. I don't. My fifth step is to study the parts I don't know. My sixth step is to relax and eat some more snacks. My plan makes me look forward to studying. It's kind of like having a party of one, or two. I give my mom some of my treats. I usually do okay on my tests. Well, unless I turn on the television and start watching it instead of studying.

**DEVELOPMENT OF IDEAS**
This writer presents a specific study plan, identifying each step clearly with signal words and explaining with some specific details. The use of the same introductory phrase throughout the essay becomes repetitive, however.

**USE OF LANGUAGE CONVENTIONS**
Sentence fragments and occasional run-on sentences reduce the effectiveness of the writing.

**Expository Essay 1: Score Summary and Rubric**                               **Score Point 2**

This expository essay addresses the prompt by explaining a unique system of studying, sure to capture readers' interest. The steps follow a logical order, but they lack details or examples to engage the reader. The last sentence, while consistent with the overall tone of the essay, weakens the impact of the controlling idea.

| | ORGANIZATION/ PROGRESSION | DEVELOPMENT OF IDEAS | USE OF LANGUAGE CONVENTIONS |
|---|---|---|---|
| **4** | • Uses appropriate structure for purpose and demands of the prompt<br>• Establishes and sustains focus, unity, and coherence via the controlling idea<br>• Controls progression with transitions showing relationships among ideas | • Employs specific and well-chosen details and examples<br>• Engages the reader through thoughtful development of ideas; may approach topic from an unusual perspective; demonstrates a deep understanding of prompt | • Shows understanding of word choice appropriate to purpose and intended tone<br>• Uses purposeful, varied, and controlled sentences<br>• Demonstrates a command of conventions so that essay is clear and effective even if it contains minor errors |
| **3** | • Uses mostly effective structure for purpose and demands of prompt<br>• Relates most ideas to controlling idea; essay is coherent though may lack overall unity<br>• Mostly controls progression of ideas with transitions | • Employs specific, appropriate details and examples that add some substance to essay<br>• Demonstrates some depth of thought, with an original rather than formulaic approach and a good understanding of the task | • Shows a basic understanding of word choice appropriate to purpose and intended tone<br>• Uses varied and generally controlled sentences<br>• Demonstrates general command of conventions; errors do not seriously affect clarity or fluency |
| **2** | • May use structure that is inappropriate to prompt; structure may not contribute to clarity of explanation<br>• May use weak or unclear controlling idea, reducing focus and coherence<br>• Has inconsistent progression of thought, with too few meaningful transitions and connections | • Lacks strong development of ideas because details are inappropriate or insufficiently developed<br>• Demonstrates little depth of thought, with a formulaic approach to the prompt and a limited understanding of the task | • Shows limited grasp of word choice, failing to establish appropriate tone<br>• Uses awkward or uncontrolled sentences, weakening essay's effectiveness<br>• Demonstrates partial command of conventions; errors may result in a lack of fluency or clarity |
| **1** | • Uses inappropriate or no obvious structure<br>• Lacks clear controlling idea, with resulting weak focus and coherence<br>• Has weak progression of thought, with lack of meaningful transitions and connections among ideas | • Lacks strong development of ideas because details and examples are inappropriate, vague, or insufficient<br>• Demonstrates lack of understanding of prompt through an overall insubstantial essay and/or a vague or confused approach | • Lacks understanding of word choice; vocabulary is imprecise or unsuitable<br>• Uses simplistic, awkward, or uncontrolled sentences, weakening essay's effectiveness<br>• Demonstrates limited or no command of conventions, resulting in a lack of fluency |

# Written Composition: Expository Essay 2

## READ

After you have done a particular task several times, you may not even think about all of the steps involved. However, when you teach someone else how to do something, it is important to remember all of the details in the right order.

## THINK

Is there a chore or household task that you would like to hand off to someone else, such as a younger sibling? If so, you need to be able to explain exactly how it is done, or else you may end up having to take the job back.

## WRITE

Write an expository essay that explains how to do a household chore or task.

**As you write your composition, remember to —**

☐ focus on a controlling idea that explains how to do a household task or chore

☐ organize your response so that each step of the process is described clearly and in order, using transitions such as *first, next,* and *finally*

☐ develop your ideas fully and thoughtfully, including appropriate facts and details to make the process clear for your readers

☐ make sure your composition is no longer than one page

**TEKS 14A, 14B, 14C, 14D, 17A, 19, 20, 21**

**ANALYZE THE PROMPT**
The prompt asks you to explain the steps involved in a familiar household chore. You should focus on the information readers would need to complete the chore themselves.

**RESPOND TO THE PROMPT**
- **Plan** by listing the chores that you have to do around the house. Choose one chore that has three or four steps that you could clearly explain in an essay.
- **Draft** your response by explaining the steps for carrying out the task in a logical order. Include specific details and examples to illustrate each step.
- **Revise** to use more precise wording, to vary your sentence types, and to add transitions.
- **Edit** your essay to correct any remaining errors in spelling, grammar, punctuation, and capitalization.

# Benchmark Composition: Expository Essay 2 **Score Point 4**

## A Fishy Situation

When I am in a cranky mood, I complain about the chores that I have to do. But, most of the time, I am pretty proud of the way I carry out my responsibilities around my house. The one task that I wouldn't mind handing over to someone else, though, is cleaning out the fish tank. I don't like fish at the best of times. When I have to be in close contact with them, I really don't like them. Because they are living creatures, however, I make sure I do a good job and follow the same steps each time.

First, before I do anything else, I fill a small bucket with water and let it stand for a few minutes to get to room temperature. It is important that the fish not suffer shock when they are placed in it.

Next, I take a net and carefully catch each fish. I gently submerge the net in the bucket and let the fish swim away. Because we have ten fish, this step takes me quite a while. But I have learned from my mistakes to be patient. Once I was hurrying and swung around too fast to make the transfer. The fish flew out of the net like a little orange missile. Luckily, it landed in the bucket, but that was a close call.

The third step is to actually clean the tank. I pull on my rubber gloves, empty the water, and begin to scrub the sides of the tank, using a special brush and cleanser. I also scrub all of the fish paraphernalia—their rocks, caves, and mermaid models that decorate the tank—making sure to rinse them thoroughly.

Finally, it is time to refill the tank. After the water is the right temperature, I do the reverse transfer, clean out the bucket for next time, and put away my tools. My last step is peeling off my rubber gloves and breathing a big sigh of relief that my dreaded job is over for another week.

**DEVELOPMENT OF IDEAS**
Within the first paragraph, the writer establishes the controlling idea of the essay, responding directly to all elements of the prompt.

**ORGANIZATION/ PROGRESSION**
Transitional words at the beginning of paragraphs signal the progression of ideas throughout the essay.

**DEVELOPMENT OF IDEAS**
The writer includes details that tell exactly how each step should be carried out and why. Providing this additional explanation is helpful to readers.

**ORGANIZATION/ PROGRESSION**
The last paragraph neatly summarizes the important steps and identifies how often the process must be done.

**Expository Essay 2: Score Summary and Rubric**                     **Score Point 4**

This expository essay is well structured, presenting the controlling idea in an introduction that also captures readers' attention. The essay also summarizes important points in a concluding paragraph. The writer uses specific and relevant details to fully respond to the prompt, creating an explanation that is both logical and engaging. The writer has strong command of conventions and sentence structure.

|   | ORGANIZATION/ PROGRESSION | DEVELOPMENT OF IDEAS | USE OF LANGUAGE CONVENTIONS |
|---|---|---|---|
| 4 | • Uses appropriate structure for purpose and demands of the prompt<br>• Establishes and sustains focus, unity, and coherence via the controlling idea<br>• Controls progression with transitions showing relationships among ideas | • Employs specific and well-chosen details and examples<br>• Engages the reader through thoughtful development of ideas; may approach topic from an unusual perspective; demonstrates a deep understanding of prompt | • Shows understanding of word choice appropriate to purpose and intended tone<br>• Uses purposeful, varied, and controlled sentences<br>• Demonstrates a command of conventions so that essay is clear and effective even if it contains minor errors |
| 3 | • Uses mostly effective structure for purpose and demands of prompt<br>• Relates most ideas to controlling idea; essay is coherent though may lack overall unity<br>• Mostly controls progression of ideas with transitions | • Employs specific, appropriate details and examples that add some substance to essay<br>• Demonstrates some depth of thought, with an original rather than formulaic approach and a good understanding of the task | • Shows a basic understanding of word choice appropriate to purpose and intended tone<br>• Uses varied and generally controlled sentences<br>• Demonstrates general command of conventions; errors do not seriously affect clarity or fluency |
| 2 | • May use structure that is inappropriate to prompt; structure may not contribute to clarity of explanation<br>• May use weak or unclear controlling idea, reducing focus and coherence<br>• Has inconsistent progression of thought, with too few meaningful transitions and connections | • Lacks strong development of ideas because details are inappropriate or insufficiently developed<br>• Demonstrates little depth of thought, with a formulaic approach to the prompt and a limited understanding of the task | • Shows limited grasp of word choice, failing to establish appropriate tone<br>• Uses awkward or uncontrolled sentences, weakening essay's effectiveness<br>• Demonstrates partial command of conventions; errors may result in a lack of fluency or clarity |
| 1 | • Uses inappropriate or no obvious structure<br>• Lacks clear controlling idea, with resulting weak focus and coherence<br>• Has weak progression of thought, with lack of meaningful transitions and connections among ideas | • Lacks strong development of ideas because details and examples are inappropriate, vague, or insufficient<br>• Demonstrates lack of understanding of prompt through an overall insubstantial essay and/or a vague or confused approach | • Lacks understanding of word choice; vocabulary is imprecise or unsuitable<br>• Uses simplistic, awkward, or uncontrolled sentences, weakening essay's effectiveness<br>• Demonstrates limited or no command of conventions, resulting in a lack of fluency |

# Benchmark Composition: Expository Essay 2

## Load Her Up!

I am an expert dishwasher loader. that's my job at home. You have to be careful when you unload. Those plates may be slippery and crash! another one bites the dust. It is important to do the job rite. First, I scrap the plates and put the left overs in the compost pale. Then I stack the large plates in the side racks on the bottom. I put cerial bowls behind them on the bottom. I put the stainless steal in the rack specially made for forks, knifes, and spoons. Next it is time to fill the top rack. I put cups and glasses upside down on the top rack. I space them real careful, that way they won't bang against each other and chip. usually before I load I fill the soap holder. Even before that first I have to unload clean dishes. I don't mind loading the dishwasher. It beats washing all of the dishes by hand, that's for sure.

**ORGANIZATION/ PROGRESSION**

The details in the central section of the essay are logically ordered. However, the organization falters at the end as the writer appears to remember details that should have been mentioned earlier in the essay.

**USE OF LANGUAGE CONVENTIONS**

Spelling and capitalization errors make this essay more difficult for readers to understand.

**Expository Essay 2: Score Summary and Rubric**                    **Score Point 2**

With more attention to detail, this essay could have been stronger, since it does convey an understanding of the prompt and include some good details. Some language is too casual *(another one bites the dust)*. Many spelling errors and the disorganization at the end of the essay indicate careless editing and a lack of planning on the part of the writer.

| | ORGANIZATION/ PROGRESSION | DEVELOPMENT OF IDEAS | USE OF LANGUAGE CONVENTIONS |
|---|---|---|---|
| **4** | • Uses appropriate structure for purpose and demands of the prompt <br> • Establishes and sustains focus, unity, and coherence via the controlling idea <br> • Controls progression with transitions showing relationships among ideas | • Employs specific and well-chosen details and examples <br> • Engages the reader through thoughtful development of ideas; may approach topic from an unusual perspective; demonstrates a deep understanding of prompt | • Shows understanding of word choice appropriate to purpose and intended tone <br> • Uses purposeful, varied, and controlled sentences <br> • Demonstrates a command of conventions so that essay is clear and effective even if it contains minor errors |
| **3** | • Uses mostly effective structure for purpose and demands of prompt <br> • Relates most ideas to controlling idea; essay is coherent though may lack overall unity <br> • Mostly controls progression of ideas with transitions | • Employs specific, appropriate details and examples that add some substance to essay <br> • Demonstrates some depth of thought, with an original rather than formulaic approach and a good understanding of the task | • Shows a basic understanding of word choice appropriate to purpose and intended tone <br> • Uses varied and generally controlled sentences <br> • Demonstrates general command of conventions; errors do not seriously affect clarity or fluency |
| **2** | • May use structure that is inappropriate to prompt; structure may not contribute to clarity of explanation <br> • May use weak or unclear controlling idea, reducing focus and coherence <br> • Has inconsistent progression of thought, with too few meaningful transitions and connections | • Lacks strong development of ideas because details are inappropriate or insufficiently developed <br> • Demonstrates little depth of thought, with a formulaic approach to the prompt and a limited understanding of the task | • Shows limited grasp of word choice, failing to establish appropriate tone <br> • Uses awkard or uncontrolled sentences, weakening essay's effectiveness <br> • Demonstrates partial command of conventions; errors may result in a lack of fluency or clarity |
| **1** | • Uses inappropriate or no obvious structure <br> • Lacks clear controlling idea, with resulting weak focus and coherence <br> • Has weak progression of thought, with lack of meaningful transitions and connections among ideas | • Lacks strong development of ideas because details and examples are inappropriate, vague, or insufficient <br> • Demonstrates lack of understanding of prompt through an overall insubstantial essay and/or a vague or confused approach | • Lacks understanding of word choice; vocabulary is imprecise or unsuitable <br> • Uses simplistic, awkward, or uncontrolled sentences, weakening essay's effectiveness <br> • Demonstrates limited or no command of conventions, resulting in a lack of fluency |

# Written Composition Practice: Personal Narrative 1

**READ**

When we look back over our lives, there are some events that
we would like to forget because they were embarrassing or sad.
There are other events that we enjoy remembering because they
made us feel happy or special.

**THINK**

What are some happy events that stand out in your memory?
Which would you like to relive? Why?

**WRITE**

Write a personal narrative that tells about an event that was
special to you and that you would like to experience again.

**As you write your composition, remember to —**

☐ focus on a controlling idea about an event in your life that you
would like to relive

☐ organize events in an order that makes sense, such as
chronological (time) order; connect ideas using transitions

☐ develop your ideas fully and thoughtfully, making it clear to
readers why the event was so special

☐ make sure your composition is no longer than one page

# Written Composition Practice: Personal Narrative 2

## READ

When we start off on a trip, even one down the street, we can never control exactly what is going to happen. Sometimes, our trip goes as planned. Other times, the unexpected happens.

## THINK

Think about trips that you have taken—short ones to school, the mall, the grocery store, or a friend's house, as well as long ones to different cities, states, or even countries. Did anything unexpected happen on any of these trips? Was the result of the surprising event good or bad?

## WRITE

Write a personal narrative telling about a trip you took during which something unexpected happened.

**As you write your composition, remember to —**

☐ focus on a controlling idea about a trip you took that had a surprising element

☐ organize events in an order that makes sense, such as chronological (time) order; connect ideas using transitions

☐ develop your ideas fully and thoughtfully, including details about the unexpected event and how you reacted

☐ make sure your composition is no longer than one page

Name _____ Date _____

# Written Composition Practice: Expository Essay 1

**READ**

One of the most useful skills that someone can have is knowing how to operate household and electronic devices, such as television remote controls, mobile phones, computers, and digital cameras. After all, the best device is useless if no one knows how to program or use it.

**THINK**

Identify a device in your household that you are able to program or operate easily. Think about the steps that someone else would need to follow in order to get successful results.

**WRITE**

Write an expository essay that explains clearly how to use a household or electronic device.

**As you write your composition, remember to —**

☐ focus on a controlling idea that explains how to use a common electronic device or other household equipment

☐ organize your ideas in a logical order, using transitions to show the connections between ideas

☐ develop your ideas fully and thoughtfully with well-chosen details and precise words

☐ make sure your composition is no longer than one page

# Written Composition Practice: Expository Essay 2

## READ

Creativity is not limited to being able to draw, paint, or do crafts. Whenever you have a vision of a finished product and take the steps to achieve that vision, you are being creative. For example, maybe you bake cookies, put together Web sites, make model airplanes, or design t-shirts.

## THINK

How do you express your creative side? Consider how you would instruct someone to do one of your creative activities. Identify materials as well as the steps that someone would need to follow to achieve the finished product.

## WRITE

Write an expository essay explaining how to do a creative activity.

**As you write your composition, remember to —**

☐ focus on a controlling idea that explains the steps and materials involved in carrying out a creative process

☐ organize your ideas in a logical order, using transitions to show the connections between ideas

☐ develop your ideas fully and thoughtfully with well-chosen details and precise words

☐ make sure your composition is no longer than one page

# Revising and Editing

# Guided Revising

**Read the following essay. Then read each question and mark the correct answer.**

*Gabriella wrote this essay about an important person in her community. She would like you to read her essay and think about the improvements she should make. When you finish reading, answer the questions that follow.*

## Mr. Santini's Bikes

(1) Mr. Santini loves to ride his bike. (2) He rides his bike to work. (3) He rides his bike to the supermarket. (4) He rides his bike to the bank, and he rides his bike to the library. (5) He rides his bike in good weather and bad. (6) His friends call him "Wheels." (7) Mr. Santini loves biking so much that he thinks everyone should ride a bike. (8) He's trying to make his wish come true in our town.

(9) One of the ways he is doing this is by fixing old bikes. (10) People give Mr. Santini their old bikes. (11) He finds broken bikes and bike parts. (12) He also puts up posters around town and has a Web site asking people to donate any used bikes. (13) He gets a lot of used or broken bikes, which he repairs and cleans up. (14) He does all this work in a big garage behind his house. (15) Sometimes he is working on ten or twelve bikes at the same time!

(16) What does he do with all these bikes? (17) He doesn't sell them. (18) He gives them away! (19) When someone needs a bike but can't afford one, that person goes to Mr. Santini's garage. (20) He helps the person pick out a bike that's the right size. (21) He also tells the new owner how to take care of the bike.

(22) Mr. Santini has been fixing bikes for ten years and giving them away. (23) Everyone in town wanted to do something to thank him for his generosity. (24) They decided to have a parade, but not just a regular parade. (25) They organized a bicycle parade! (26) Anyone with a bike, especially anyone with a "Santini Bike," gathered in the center of town. (27) Other people lined up along the sides of the street. (28) Many of them held signs that said, "Thank you, Mr. Santini!" (29) Then all the bike riders pedaled through town. (30) Mr. Santini's wish came true.

**GO ON**

1 Gabriella thinks sentences 2–4 sound too repetitive. What is the best way for her to combine them?

A He rides his bike to work, the supermarket, the bank, and to the library.

B He rides his bike to work, to the supermarket, to the bank, and to the library.

C He rides his bike to work and to the supermarket, and he rides his bike to the bank and to the library.

D He rides his bike to work, and he also rides his bike to the supermarket, the bank, and the library.

> **EXPLANATION:** The sentences can be combined so that the subject (*he*), verb (*rides*), and object (*his bike*) are used only once. The correct answer is **B**.
> • **A** is incorrect. The preposition *to* provides clarity and should be placed before each item in the series, not just the first and last items.
> • **C** and **D** are incorrect because they unnecessarily repeat the subject, verb, and object (*he rides his bike*).

**TEKS 14C**

2 To connect to sentence 12 and improve sentence variety, which transition word or phrase should Gabriella add to the beginning of sentence 13?

F After

G At first

H As a result

J In conclusion

> **EXPLANATION:** Mr. Santini gets a lot of used or broken bikes as a result of his requests for donations. The correct answer is **H**.
> • **F** is incorrect. Adding the conjunction *After* to the beginning of the sentence creates a dependent clause: *After he gets a lot of used and broken bikes.* Combining this with another dependent clause (*which he repairs and cleans up*) makes an ungrammatical sentence.
> • **G** is incorrect because the paragraph does not describe a sequence of events.
> • **J** is incorrect. Sentence 13 does not provide a final summary of information.

**TEKS 14C**

GO ON

**3** Gabriella wants to add a sentence to help support the ideas in the third paragraph (sentences 16–21). Which sentence could best follow sentence 21?

**A** Bike riding is an excellent form of exercise.

**B** Mr. Santini knows a lot about fixing things.

**C** Taking good care of a bike is very important.

**D** Mr. Santini is a very kind and generous person.

> **EXPLANATION:** The details in the paragraph support the idea that Mr. Santini is a kind and generous person. The correct answer is **D**.
> - **A** and **B** are incorrect because they do not follow from and support the main ideas in the paragraph.
> - **C** is incorrect. Although it is related to sentence 21, it provides unnecessary information that distracts readers from the main idea of the paragraph, which is about Mr. Santini's kindness and generosity.

**TEKS 14C**

**4** To clarify meaning, what is the best way for Gabriella to rewrite the ideas in sentence 22?

**F** Mr. Santini has been fixing bikes and giving them away for ten years.

**G** Mr. Santini has been fixing bikes for ten years, and he also gives them away.

**H** Mr. Santini fixes bikes and gives them away. He has been doing this for ten years.

**J** Mr. Santini has been fixing bikes for ten years. After he fixes them, he gives them away.

> **EXPLANATION:** The sentence should clarify that Mr. Santini has been fixing bikes as well as giving them away for ten years. The correct answer is **F**.
> - **G** and **J** are incorrect. In this context, it does not make sense to separate the act of fixing the bikes from the act of giving them away.
> - **H** is incorrect. The second and third paragraphs already describe how Mr. Santini fixes bikes and gives them away. The topic sentence of the fourth paragraph should immediately introduce the idea that he has been doing this for ten years, which explains the reason for the parade.

**TEKS 14C**

STOP

Name _____ Date _____

# Revising Practice 1

**Read the following essay. Then read each question and mark the correct answer.**

*Paola wrote this essay about a famous world event. She would like you to read her paper and think about the improvements she should make. When you finish reading, answer the questions that follow.*

## Let the Games Begin!

(1) The Olympic Games are the biggest sporting event in the world. (2) The first Olympics were held in Greece over 2,000 years ago. (3) Athletes from many countries come to compete in the Summer and Winter Games. (4) There are about 400 events in 33 different sports. (5) Winners in each event get a gold, silver, or bronze medal. (6) The modern Summer Games started in 1896.

(7) The Summer Games happen every four years in different cities. (8) An international committee votes to choose which city will host the games. (9) The United States has hosted four Summer Olympics. (10) The United States has hosted the Summer Olympics more than any other country. (11) Some Summer Games events include basketball, swimming, and gymnastics.

(12) The Winter Games began in 1924. (13) They are also held every four years. (14) They are always in a place that has mountains and snow for skiing. (15) Other sports at the Winter Games include figure skating and ice hockey.

(16) Approximately 13,000 athletes compete in the Summer and Winter Olympics. (17) Where do they all stay? (18) Each city builds an Olympic village for all the athletes and coaches. (19) It's like a small city within a city.

(20) The Olympic Games have many traditions. (21) One is the Olympic Torch relay. (22) Runners take turns carrying a torch from Greece to the Olympic stadium. (23) The last runner lights a huge fire that burns during the Games. (24) Another tradition is the Olympic flag. (25) It has five rings of different colors, each one representing an area of the world. (26) You can also see the flags of many countries. (27) The Olympics are an important event that unites nations.

GO ON

Name _____ Date _____

**1** Which sentences should Paola rearrange to improve the organization of her essay?

**A** Move sentence 5 so that it follows sentence 2

**B** Move sentence 5 so that it comes before sentence 1

**C** Move sentence 2 so that it follows sentence 5

**D** Move sentence 4 so that it follows sentence 5

**2** How should Paola rewrite the ideas in sentence 7 to make her meaning clearer?

**F** Every four years, the Summer Games happen in different cities.

**G** On each fourth year, the Summer Games happen in a different city.

**H** The Summer Games happen every four years, each time in a different city.

**J** The Summer Games happen in different cities, and they occur four years apart.

**3** Paola thinks sentences 9 and 10 sound choppy and repetitive. What is the best way for her to combine them?

**A** The United States has hosted four Summer Olympics, more than any other country.

**B** The country to host the most Summer Olympics is the United States; it has hosted four.

**C** The United States has been chosen to host four Summer Olympics—this is more than any other country.

**D** The most any country has hosted the Summer Olympics is four times, and this was done by the United States.

**4** How can Paola best revise sentences 13 and 14 to compare and contrast the Summer and Winter Olympics?

**F** The Winter Games are also held every four years. The host city is also chosen by committee, yet the games are held in a place with mountains and snow for skiing.

**G** Both the Summer and Winter Games are held every four years. Although the Winter Games are held in an area that has mountains and snow for skiing, the host city is chosen by committee.

**H** Like the Summer Games, the Winter Games are held every four years in a host city chosen by committee. However, the Winter Games must take place in an area that has mountains and snow for skiing.

**J** On one hand, the Summer and Winter Games are held every four years in a city chosen by committee. On the other hand, the Winter Games must take place in an area that has mountains and snow for skiing.

**5** To connect to sentence 20, which transition word or phrase should Paola add to the beginning of sentence 21?

**A** First
**B** Instead
**C** For example
**D** On the contrary

**6** Which sentence should Paola delete from the last paragraph because it does not relate to the main idea?

**F** Sentence 23
**G** Sentence 25
**H** Sentence 26
**J** Sentence 27

# Revising Practice 2

Read the following essay. Then read each question and mark the correct answer.

*Katrina wrote this essay about ways in which students can protect the environment. She would like you to read her paper and think about the improvements she should make. When you finish reading, answer the questions that follow.*

## Ways to Protect the Environment

(1) Scientists tell us that the environment is in trouble. (2) Landfills are running out of room for trash. (3) There are many things students can do to reduce greenhouse gases and pollution.

(4) First, students can ride their bikes or walk to school when possible instead of getting a ride in a car. (5) Carbon dioxide makes up part of the greenhouse gases. (6) Cars release carbon dioxide. (7) If students walk or ride their bikes, there is less carbon dioxide released into the air. (8) This helps the environment, because less carbon dioxide means less greenhouse gases.

(9) Students can improve the environment through recycling. (10) There are many things students throw away every day that can be recycled. (11) Students can collect aluminum soda cans and plastic water bottles. (12) They also can collect paper in their classrooms. (13) Imagine if all of the cans, bottles, and paper in schools were recycled. (14) Some benefits of recycling include less trash, fewer trees used for paper, and fewer landfills.

(15) Finally, students can help the environment by planting trees. (16) Trees help the environment because they use carbon dioxide and release oxygen. (17) Furthermore, trees provide shade. (18) If homes and buildings are shaded, they use less electricity, which also helps the environment. (19) Students can join the Arbor Club. (20) The Arbor Club plants trees at schools and businesses in our community.

(21) Walking or riding a bike to school, recycling, and planting trees are just a few of the ways that students can help the environment. (22) These efforts can help reduce greenhouse gases and garbage.

GO ON ➡

**1** Katrina wants to add to the ideas in sentences 1–3. Which sentence could best follow sentence 1?

**A** Students riding their scooters to school will lessen pollution.

**B** Tree clearing and fuel burning are harming our air quality.

**C** Scientists disagree about the causes and effects of environmental change.

**D** Some people believe that the environment will take care of itself.

**2** In the second paragraph (sentences 4–8), which sentences should Katrina rearrange to clarify ideas for her audience?

**F** Move sentence 7 so that it follows sentence 8

**G** Move sentence 7 so that it follows sentence 3

**H** Move sentence 8 so that it follows sentence 4

**J** Move sentence 6 so that it follows sentence 4

**3** Katrina wants to improve the transitions between paragraphs in her essay. What is the best way for her to revise sentence 9?

**A** Specifically, students can help the environment through recycling.

**B** One way students can help the environment is through recycling.

**C** Recycling is another way in which students can help the environment.

**D** Indeed, recycling is an important way in which students can help the environment.

**4** Katrina wants to replace *help the environment* in sentence 16 with a more precise phrase. Which phrase should she use to describe trees?

**F** are notable

**G** benefit our planet

**H** improve air quality

**J** change the atmosphere

**5** How should Katrina combine sentences 19 and 20 to relate these details more clearly to her main idea?

**A** Students can join the Arbor Club, which plants trees at schools and businesses in our community.

**B** Students can join the Arbor Club; the Arbor Club plants trees at schools and businesses in our community.

**C** The Arbor Club plants trees at schools and businesses; students can help plant trees in our community when they join this club.

**D** The Arbor Club plants trees at schools and businesses in our community, and students can plant trees too when they join this club.

**6** Katrina wants to end her essay with a final thought that expands on her main idea. What is the best sentence to add after sentence 22?

**F** Greenhouse gases and garbage harm the environment.

**G** Reducing greenhouse gases and garbage is how students can help the environment.

**H** If students in more schools took these easy steps, they could make a big difference.

**J** After they follow these steps, there are many other things students can do to make a difference.

STOP

Name _____ Date _____

# Guided Editing

---

**Read the following personal narrative. Then read each question and mark the correct answer.**

---

*Eli wrote this personal narrative about the best gift he ever received. He would like you to read his narrative and think about the corrections he should make. When you finish reading, answer the questions that follow.*

## A Surprise Gift

(1) I was eating my lunch when my mother walked into the kitchen. (2) "We're going to visit Grandma for two weeks" she said. (3) I froze in mid-chew. (4) My grandmother lives on a small farm about eight hundred miles away in the middle of nowhere. (5) How was I going to survive two whole weeks at my grandmother's house?

(6) We arrived at my grandmother's farm, she was waiting for us on the front porch. (7) She was holding something that was black and wriggling. (8) I got out of the car, and at the same time, Grandma put down the wriggling thing. (9) Then it started to run toward me. (10) It was a puppy! (11) I sat on the ground, and the puppy crawls all over me and licks my face. (12) It was so excited and wiggled so much that it felt like having three puppies all over me.

(13) "I was afraid you would be bored here. (14) I talked to your parents and they said I could get you a puppy," Grandma said. (15) "You can start training the puppy while you're here, and then take him home with you." (16) "Wow, thanks!" I exclaimed, totally surprised that Grandma, as a result of managing her farm, would have the time and foresight to consider my boredom.

(17) I named my puppy dizzy because he likes to jump up and down in a circle. (18) It makes you dizzy to look at him! (19) We spent the whole two weeks together. (20) My dad helped me teach him how to sit and stay. (21) We played fetch in the fields and helped out on the farm together, and he slept with me every night. (22) Every day was fun and busy. (23) I can't believe it, but I didn't miss home at all!

**1** What change, if any, should be made in sentence 2?

**A** Insert a comma after *weeks*

**B** Change *to visit* to **on a visit with**

**C** Change *We're going to visit Grandma* to **Grandma will be visited by us**

**D** Make no change

> **EXPLANATION:** A comma should be placed at the end of the words someone says and before the closing quotation marks. The correct answer is **A.**
> - **B** is incorrect because it suggests going somewhere with Grandma rather than visiting her at her home.
> - **C** is incorrect because using the passive voice sounds awkward.
> - **D** is incorrect. A change is necessary.

**TEKS 14D, 19A, 19B, 20B**

**2** What change should be made in sentence 6?

**F** Change *grandmother's* to **Grandmother's**

**G** Delete the comma after *farm*

**H** Change *at* to **to**

**J** Change *We* to **When we**

> **EXPLANATION:** Sentence 6 has two independent clauses joined by a comma; it is a run-on. Adding the subordinating conjunction *When* creates a correctly written complex sentence. The correct answer is **J.**
> - **F** is incorrect. *Grandmother* should be capitalized only if it is the name by which she is called (like *Grandma*).
> - **G** is incorrect. The comma is needed between the two clauses.
> - **H** is incorrect because *arrived at* is the correct phrase in standard English.

**TEKS 14D, 19A, 20B**

**3** What change, if any, should be made in sentence 11?

**A** Insert a comma after *me*

**B** Change *sat* to **sit**

**C** Change *crawls* and *licks* to **crawled** and **licked**

**D** Make no change

> **EXPLANATION:** The narrative is told in the past tense. The verbs that describe the puppy's actions should also be in the past tense. The correct answer is **C.**
> - **A** is incorrect. A comma should not separate the two verbs that describe what the puppy does.
> - **B** is incorrect because all the action in the narrative is described in the past tense.
> - **D** is incorrect. A change is necessary.

**TEKS 14D, 19, 20B**

**4** What change should be made in sentence 16?

**F** Change *exclaimed* to **exclamed**

**G** Insert a comma after the exclamation point

**H** Replace the exclamation point with a comma

**J** Change *as a result of* to **in addition to**

> **EXPLANATION:** The phrase *as a result of* signals cause and effect, but there is no cause-effect relationship between Grandma's thinking about Eli's boredom and her management of the farm. A transitional phrase is needed to show Eli's surprise that Grandma took the time to be so thoughtful despite her busy life on the farm. The correct answer is **J.**
> - **F** is incorrect. Changing the spelling of *exclaimed* will create an error.
> - **G** and **H** are incorrect because the dialogue is punctuated correctly.

**TEKS 14D, 19A, 20B, 21**

**GO ON**

**5** What change, if any, should be made in sentence 17?

**A** Change *in* to **about in**
**B** Change *dizzy* to **Dizzy**
**C** Change *down* to **jump down**
**D** Make no change

> **EXPLANATION:** *Dizzy* refers to the name Eli gave to his dog, so it should be capitalized. The correct answer is **B**.
> - **A** is incorrect because two prepositions are unnecessary to describe the dog's actions.
> - **C** is incorrect. Since *up* and *down* both modify *jump*, it is unnecessary to repeat the verb.
> - **D** is incorrect. A change is necessary.

**TEKS 14D, 19A, 20**

**6** What change should be made in sentence 21?

**F** Change *fetch* to **fech**
**G** Change *sleeped* to **slept**
**H** Delete the comma after *together*
**J** Change *and he sleeped* to **although he sleeped**

> **EXPLANATION:** *Sleep* is an irregular verb; its past-tense form is *slept*. The correct answer is **G**.
> - **F** is incorrect. Changing the spelling of *fetch* will create an error.
> - **H** is incorrect. The comma correctly separates the two independent clauses.
> - **J** is incorrect. The coordinating conjunction *and* correctly connects the two clauses. No evidence suggests that the subordinating conjunction *although* is needed to show a contrast.

**TEKS 14D, 19A, 20B, 21**

# Editing Practice 1

> **Read the following personal narrative. Then read each question and mark the correct answer.**

*Edwin wrote this personal narrative about a life-changing event. He would like you to read his narrative and look for the corrections he should make. When you finish reading, answer the questions that follow.*

## A New Talent

(1) Braking my leg was one of the best things that ever happened to me. (2) I know that sounds crazy, but before it happened, I thought playing football was the only thing I was good at. (3) I was so wrong!

(4) It used to be that, football was my whole life. (5) I'm talented at it and have dreamed about playing for the nfl since I was a little kid. (6) I can snatch a football right out of the air, and I'm fast. (7) For example, one day at practice I was running to catch the ball and got knocked down hard. (8) When I tried to stand, the pain was terrible! (9) Later, at the hospital, the doctor told me I had broken my leg and I couldn't play football for eight weeks. (10) What was I going to do?

(11) When nothing was cheering me up, my little sister said "Stop moping already! Color with me. It's really fun!" (12) I took some paper and crayons and started to draw. (13) Suddenly, I realized that one hour had gone by, but it felt like it had only been a few minutes! (14) I had completely lost me in the process of putting shapes and colors on paper, and the time had just flown by.

(15) My parents gave me artist's pencils and paper, and I drew every day. (16) I showed some of my pictures to the school art teacher, and she put two of my drawings in a contest. (17) "You're becoming quite the artist. Keep it up!" she said. (18) Me? (19) An artist?

(20) Tomorrow I start football practice again, and I'm excited to get on the field and be with my teammates. (21) However, this time I know that football won't be the only thing I do in my free time. (22) My broken leg gave me the chance to find something else that I'm good at.

**1** What change, if any, should be made in sentence 1?

   **A** Change *Braking* to **Breaking**
   **B** Change *that* to **than**
   **C** Change *things* to **thing**
   **D** Make no change

**2** What change should be made in sentence 4?

   **F** Change *whole* to **hole**
   **G** Change *was* to **were**
   **H** Delete the comma after *that*
   **J** Change *used to* to **use to**

**3** What change should be made in sentence 5?

   **A** Change *nfl* to **NFL**
   **B** Change *have* to **has**
   **C** Change *since* to **when**
   **D** Change *talented* to **tallented**

**4** What change should be made in sentence 7?

   **F** Insert a comma after *ball*
   **G** Change *For example* to **However**
   **H** Change *down* to **forward**
   **J** Change *at* to **near**

**5** What change, if any, should be made in sentence 11?

   **A** Change *It's* to **Its**
   **B** Change *was* to **were**
   **C** Insert a comma after *said*
   **D** Make no change

**6** What change should be made in sentence 14?

   **F** Change *in* to **by**
   **G** Change *me* to **myself**
   **H** Change *flown* to **flew**
   **J** Change the comma to a semicolon

# Editing Practice 2

**Read the following personal narrative. Then read each question and mark the correct answer.**

*Darnell wrote this personal narrative about helping out at home. He would like you to read his paper and think about the corrections he should make. When you finish reading, answer the questions that follow.*

## Taking Charge?

(1) My dad says I should give Mom a break and help take care of my little brother, Mikey. (2) So I promise I will, even though I'm not thrilled about it. (3) Sometimes the little guy gets sticky fingerprints on my homework or tries to eat it. (4) I probably shouldn't get mad since he's just a baby.

(5) Today I am in my room, doing homework. (6) Suddenly, I here the phone ring. (7) "Will you get that, please?" Mom yells from the kitchen.

(8) I run to pick up the phone. (9) It's my grandpa, calling from New York. (10) "It's grandpa Evans," I call to Mom. (11) "What does he want?" she calls back.

(12) He tells me what to tell Mom, and she tells me what to say back. (13) Finally I say, "Mom, talk to Grandpa and I'll feed Mikey!" (14) Mom takes the phone, and gives me Mikey's spoon and a dish of squash.

(15) Mikey looks at me, waiting. (16) I scoop up some squash and mimic Mom. (17) I aim the spoon at his mouth and say, "Here comes the airplane!" (18) Mikey takes a mouthful of squash and then, like a volcano, shoots it back at me!

(19) Although I am busy cleaning up, Mikey picks up the spoon and WHAM, squash flies across the room. (20) I think, "This kid will make the NBA!"

(21) Mikey throws spoonful after spoonful. (22) Before I can stop him, squash is everywhere. (23) Our cat Misty jumps out of the way as squash lands near her on the floor. (24) Just then, Mom walks in and slips on a glob of squash! (25) She looks up at me, covered in food. (26) We both look at Mikey, who smiles and says proudly, "Quach!" (27) Mom laughs, "Mikey's learned a new word!" (28) Mikey grins as he repeats his new word; *quach* . . . short for squash.

**GO ON**

**1** What change, if any, should be made in sentence 4?

    **A** Change *probably shouldn't* to **shouldn't probably**

    **B** Change *since* to **but**

    **C** Insert a comma after *since*

    **D** Make no change

**2** What change should be made in sentence 6?

    **F** Change *Suddenly* to **Consequently**

    **G** Change *here* to **hear**

    **H** Delete the comma after *Suddenly*

    **J** Change *ring* to **rings**

**3** What change, if any, should be made in sentence 10?

    **A** Change *It's* to **Its**

    **B** Change *grandpa* to **Grandpa**

    **C** Delete the comma after *Evans*

    **D** Make no change

**4** What change should be made in sentence 14?

    **F** Change *takes* to **took**

    **G** Insert a comma after *spoon*

    **H** Delete the comma after *phone*

    **J** Change *dish* to **ditch**

**5** What change should be made in sentence 19?

    **A** Change *flies* to **fly**

    **B** Change *Although* to **While**

    **C** Replace the comma after *WHAM* with a semicolon

    **D** Enclose *squash flies across the room* in parentheses

**6** What change, if any, should be made in sentence 28?

    **F** Change *as* to **during**

    **G** Change *repeats* to **repeated**

    **H** Change the semicolon to a colon

    **J** Make no change

STOP

# Part II

## Texas Write Source
## Assessments

# Pretest

## Part 1: Basic Elements of Writing

> **Questions 1–12: Read each sentence. Choose the best way to write the underlined part of the sentence. Fill in the circle of the correct answer on your answer document.**

**1** Nate <u>ran into the field and catched</u> a butterfly in his net.

   **A** runned into the field and catched
   **B** ran into the field and caught
   **C** runned into the field and caught
   **D** Make no change

**2** Caroline and Trey took off their shoes <u>although</u> they wanted to go wading.

   **F** if
   **G** because
   **H** hence
   **J** Make no change

**3** On our hike, the rain <u>fell steady</u> for more than an hour.

   **A** fell steadily
   **B** fell steadier
   **C** falled steady
   **D** Make no change

**4** That was <u>the nice campground</u> I've ever seen!

   **F** the nicest campground
   **G** the nice campgrounds
   **H** the nicer campground
   **J** Make no change

**5** We pitched our tent <u>between two birch trees</u>.

   **A** around two birch trees
   **B** among two birch trees
   **C** through two birch trees
   **D** Make no change

**6** Porcupines have quills to <u>protect themselves</u> from other animals.

   **F** protect itself
   **G** protect themself
   **H** protect itselves
   **J** Make no change

**7** By tomorrow, we <u>were ready</u> to return home.

   **A** are ready
   **B** will be ready
   **C** being ready
   **D** Make no change

**8** Andrew and I enjoyed watching <u>a beautiful sunset</u>.

   **F** an beautiful sunset
   **G** a beauty sunset
   **H** a beautifuler sunset
   **J** Make no change

**9** When the rain started, we <u>walked quick</u> to the car.

   **A** walked quicker

   **B** walked quickest

   **C** walked quickly

   **D** Make no change

**10** Fernanda refuses to go fishing <u>but</u> we go swimming, too.

   **F** unless

   **G** after

   **H** since

   **J** Make no change

**11** My sister and I <u>likes to go</u> rock climbing.

   **A** likes to goes

   **B** like to go

   **C** like to going

   **D** Make no change

**12** <u>Uncle Raymond is</u> an avid birdwatcher and photographer.

   **F** Uncle Raymond am

   **G** Uncle Raymond are

   **H** Uncle Raymond being

   **J** Make no change

---

**Questions 13–18: Read each question and fill in the circle of the correct answer on your answer document.**

---

**13** Which is a complete sentence written correctly?

   **A** The Wright brothers' first flight on December 17, 1903.

   **B** Took place near Kitty Hawk, North Carolina.

   **C** The plane flew for 12 seconds and traveled 120 feet.

   **D** Name of the Wright brothers' plane being *Flyer*.

**14** Which is a run-on sentence that should be written as two sentences?

   **F** The Panama Canal connects the Atlantic Ocean with the Pacific Ocean.

   **G** Until November 3, 1903, Panama was part of Colombia.

   **H** President Theodore Roosevelt wanted to build the Panama Canal.

   **J** Construction began in 1903 the canal opened in 1914.

**15** Which is the best way to combine these two sentences?

> The first European to visit Hawaii was Captain James Cook.
>
> Captain Cook visited Hawaii in 1778.

   **A** The first European in 1778 to visit Hawaii was Captain James Cook.

   **B** In 1778, Captain James Cook became the first European to visit Hawaii.

   **C** Captain James Cook, the first European, visited Hawaii in 1778.

   **D** The first European to visit Hawaii in 1778 was Captain James Cook.

GO ON

**16** Which is the best way to combine these two sentences?

> Hawaii became a U.S. territory in 1898.
>
> Hawaii did not become a state until 1959.

**F** Hawaii became a U.S. territory in 1898, but it did not become a state until 1959.

**G** Hawaii became a U.S. territory in 1898, it became a state in 1959.

**H** Hawaii became a U.S. territory in 1898, so it did not become a state until 1959.

**J** In 1898 Hawaii became a U.S. territory, in 1959 it became a state.

**17** Which is an interrogative sentence that should end with a question mark?

**A** One of the world's first civilizations began in China more than 6,000 years ago

**B** Around 1200 B.C., a system of writing was developed by the Shang Dynasty

**C** In 1271, how did the Mongol invaders take control of China

**D** The Chinese invented many things, including paper, ink, and gunpowder

**18** Which is a declarative sentence that should end with a period?

**F** What is your favorite vegetable

**G** I've never tasted a rutabaga

**H** Can you eat broccoli uncooked

**J** Look at that wonderful salad

Questions 19–20: A student wrote this paragraph about working at a food co-op. It may need some changes or corrections. Read the paragraph. Then read each question. Fill in the circle of the correct answer on your answer document.

**At the Co-op**

Last Saturday Dad and I worked at the food co-op. Great food can be bought at the co-op because we're members, but we have to work there once a month. That day we arrived at ten o'clock. Several guys were unloading crates of vegetables from a truck. Two women were pushing carts filled with cartons of milk. Dad and I started opening big bags of potatoes, carrots, and onions. The first two hours of work flew by, and then Joel showed up.

**19** What type of paragraph is this?

**A** expository
**B** persuasive
**C** response to a text
**D** narrative

**20** Which detail sentence could best be added just before the last sentence in this paragraph?

**F** The co-op is located on Sun Street.
**G** Then we spent an hour stacking canned goods.
**H** I saw one of my friends walk by.
**J** The price for a loaf of bread is only $1.75!

GO ON

# Part 2: Proofreading and Editing

> **Questions 21–30: Read the passages. Choose the best way to write each underlined part. Fill in the circle of the correct answer on your answer document.**

This year, we read many poems written by the famous poet,

<u>T.S. Eliot</u>. My favorites were originally published in a book called
  **21**

<u>"Old Possum's Book of practical Cats"</u>. This book was first published in
  **22**

1939. It was an <u>imediate</u> hit with adults and children alike. Everyone in
     **23**

our class really enjoyed this book.

    <u>Similarly, my sister says</u> reading poetry is a waste of time.
     **24**

<u>But she was told by me</u> that Eliot's poems are easy and fun to read.
  **25**

They aren't a waste of time at all.

**21 A** t s Eliot
   **B** T. S. Eliot
   **C** TS. Eliot
   **D** Make no change

**22 F** *Old Possum's Book of Practical Cats*
   **G** *Old Possum's Book of practical Cats*
   **H** "old Possum's Book of Practical Cats"
   **J** Make no change

**23 A** immediately
   **B** immediate
   **C** most immediate
   **D** Make no change

**24 F** Likewise, my sister says
   **G** On the other hand, my sister says
   **H** For instance, my sister says
   **J** Make no change

**25 A** But she was told by I
   **B** But I told she
   **C** But I told her
   **D** Make no change

June 4 2011
**26**

<u>Dear Kirsten.</u>
**27**

My friends and I just went to see the musical *Cats*. It was

incredible! The music was <u>really beautiful, and</u> the songs were
**28**

pretty funny, too. Afterwards my mother bought me a book called

<u>"Great American Musicals."</u> You have got to see it!
**29**

I <u>can't hardly wait</u> until your visit!
**30**

Yours,

Sophia

**26 F** June, 4, 2011
**G** June 4, 2011
**H** June 4. 2011
**J** Make no change

**27 A** dear Kirsten.
**B** Dear Kirsten
**C** Dear Kirsten,
**D** Make no change

**28 F** really beautiful and
**G** really beautiful; and
**H** really beautiful. And
**J** Make no change

**29 A** Great American Musicals.
**B** Great American Musicals.
**C** 'Great American Musicals.'
**D** Make no change

**30 F** can hardly wait
**G** hardly can't wait
**H** cannot hardly wait
**J** Make no change

GO ON

## Part 3: Writing                                    **Narrative**

### READ

During the school year we participate in many activities and have many different experiences. Many of these activities and experiences are similar to things we've done in previous years at school, but some are new to us, leading us to look at things differently or to think about things in new ways.

### THINK

Think about a new activity you participated in or a new experience you had this year that you enjoyed.

What did you do? Why did you particularly enjoy this new experience?

### WRITE

Write a narrative essay describing a new activity or experience you enjoyed.

*As you write your composition, remember to —*

☐ focus on a controlling idea that reflects something you did that was new and enjoyable

☐ organize your ideas logically and link them with transitions

☐ include appropriate facts and details about the event and communicate its importance

☐ make sure your composition is no longer than one page

# Progress Test 1

## Part 1: Basic Elements of Writing

Questions 1–12: Read each sentence. Choose the best way to write the underlined part of the sentence. Fill in the circle of the correct answer on your answer document.

**1** The Great Depression of the 1930s was a <u>difficultest</u> time for the United States.

   A more difficult
   B difficult
   C difficulter
   D Make no change

**2** For nearly ten years, <u>many Americans was</u> unemployed, hungry, and even homeless.

   F many Americans are
   G many Americans is
   H many Americans were
   J Make no change

**3** Schools closed all over the country; <u>consequently</u>, 200,000 teachers lost their jobs.

   A indeed
   B however
   C for example
   D Make no change

**4** When any job was advertised, hundreds of men <u>quick lined up</u> to apply.

   F quicker lined up
   G quickly lined up
   H quickest lined up
   J Make no change

**5** Whole families waited in line for hours <u>to get</u> a bit of soup and bread.

   A to got
   B to getting
   C to gotten
   D Make no change

**6** Many Americans wanted the government to help <u>they</u>.

   F it
   G them
   H themselves
   J Make no change

**7** Some people even blamed Herbert Hoover, <u>who was the president</u> at the beginning of the Great Depression.

   A which was the president
   B whose the president
   C that was the president
   D Make no change

**8** In 1932, Franklin Delano Roosevelt <u>has elected</u> president.

   F is elected
   G was elected
   H had elected
   J Make no change

GO ON ➡

**9** President Roosevelt told the country about his <u>creatively plan</u> to rescue the country from the Depression.

   **A** his creativest plan
   **B** his plan creatively
   **C** his creative plan
   **D** Make no change

**10** Thousands of men <u>was given</u> jobs planting trees, building bridges, and constructing roads.

   **F** were given
   **G** is given
   **H** being given
   **J** Make no change

**11** Roosevelt's programs helped many people feel <u>best</u>, but recovery was slow.

   **A** gooder
   **B** better
   **C** more good
   **D** Make no change

**12** The end of the Depression finally <u>coming</u> in 1939.

   **F** comes
   **G** comed
   **H** came
   **J** Make no change

---

**Questions 13–18: Read each question and fill in the circle of the correct answer on your answer document.**

---

**13** Which is a complete sentence written correctly?

   **A** Eating chips and drinking soda all night long.
   **B** Davis and his friends from soccer.
   **C** Ignoring the butterflies in her stomach, Emma asked Ravi to dance.
   **D** Ravi did not know how to dance he said yes anyway.

**14** Which is a run-on sentence and should be written as two sentences?

   **F** Elijah and Alana requested a rap song the D.J. had only hip hop.
   **G** Sarah, that new girl, really knows how to dance.
   **H** Where on earth did you get that cool shirt?
   **J** The dance is at eight o'clock this Friday night.

**15** Which is the best way to combine these two sentences?

> The dance starts at eight o'clock.
>
> The dance is tonight.

   **A** The dance starts at eight o'clock and the dance is tonight.
   **B** The dance starts at eight o'clock, the dance is tonight.
   **C** The dance starts at eight o'clock tonight.
   **D** The dance is at eight o'clock starting tonight.

GO ON

**16** Which is the best way to combine these two sentences?

> My friend Logan called. My friend Logan said he would meet me there.

**F** My friend Logan called and said he would meet me there.

**G** My friend Logan called he said he would meet me there.

**H** My friend Logan called; Logan said he would meet me there.

**J** My friend Logan called and met me there.

**17** Which is an interrogative sentence and should end with a question mark?

**A** It would be great if your brother could give us a ride

**B** Can you ask him if he's busy

**C** Tell him we also need a ride home

**D** I wish I knew if he was going to the dance

**18** Which is an imperative sentence that should end with a period?

**F** Do you want to dance

**G** You are so funny sometimes

**H** Ms. Davis told me she was going to dance, too

**J** Call me as soon as you get home

---

**Questions 19–20:** A student wrote this paragraph about a camping trip. It may need some changes or corrections. Read the paragraph. Then read each question. Fill in the circle of the correct answer on your answer document.

---

### Drizzly Days

(1) This summer my family went camping at Acadia National Park. (2) The car ride was long, but Mom had packed some fun games. (3) We planned the meals, packed our bags, and took off for a week on Maine's beautiful coast. (4) When we got to the campground, it was nearly dark. (5) We could barely see as we set up our tents and gathered firewood to make dinner. (6) We woke up the next morning ready for a hike and a picnic on the beach. (7) It was pouring rain, so we decided to check out the local shops and museums instead. (8) Little did we know it would rain every day that week!

**19** Which detail could best be added just before sentence 8?

**A** My little brothers are actually allergic to sun block.

**B** The waves were huge.

**C** We weren't used to the waves.

**D** The harbor towns were beautiful, even in the rain.

**20** Which two sentences should be switched to organize the paragraph better?

**F** sentences 1 and 2

**G** sentences 2 and 3

**H** sentences 4 and 5

**J** sentences 5 and 6

GO ON

# Part 2: Proofreading and Editing

> **Questions 21–30: Read the passages. Choose the best way to write each underlined part. Fill in the circle of the correct answer on your answer document.**

The Spanish language has many words that are <u>simmilar</u> to
**21**

<u>english words</u>. For example, the Spanish words *frutas* and *vegetales*
**22**

are very close to the words *fruits* and *vegetables*. <u>An amount</u> of words
**23**

are spelled exactly the same in both languages, <u>such as the following</u>
**24**

soda, chocolate, pasta, and auto. Yesterday my mom said, <u>"That dog is</u>
**25**

<u>loco"</u>! *Loco* is a Spanish word meaning "crazy."

**21 A** simillar
   **B** similar
   **C** simmiler
   **D** Make no change

**22 F** English words
   **G** english wordes
   **H** English Words
   **J** Make no change

**23 A** A amount
   **B** A mount
   **C** A number
   **D** Make no change

**24 F** such as, the following.
   **G** such as the following:
   **H** such as, the following,
   **J** Make no change

**25 A** "That dog is *loco!*"
   **B** 'That dog is *loco!*'
   **C** That dog is *loco!*
   **D** Make no change

<u>Hello my</u> name is Terrence Camden. You should vote for me for
**26**

class president because I will <u>work hardly</u> for you and your needs. For
**27**

example, is your back breaking from the strain of carrying all those

books in your <u>book bags?</u> If you vote for me, I will lead the campaign
**28**

for <u>nicer newer and bigger</u> lockers. <u>Together can make</u> this school
**29**                                              **30**

better! Vote for Terrence Camden!

**26 F** Hello. my
   **G** Hello My
   **H** Hello, my
   **J** Make no change

**27 A** work more hard
   **B** work hardlier
   **C** work hard
   **D** Make no change

**28 F** book bags!
   **G** book bags.
   **H** book bags,
   **J** Make no change

**29 A** nicer, newer, and, bigger
   **B** nicer, newer, and bigger
   **C** nicer newer, and bigger
   **D** Make no change

**30 F** Together we can make
   **G** Together can making
   **H** Can make together
   **J** Make no change

**GO ON**

## Part 3: Writing                                          Expository

### READ

All of us have a favorite room. It may be a bedroom, a kitchen, a family room, or even a garage. Your favorite room might not even be in the house or apartment where you live.

### THINK

Think of your favorite room. What does it look like? Try to remember details of its size, its shape, and the arrangement of objects or furniture in it.

### WRITE

Write an expository essay explaining in detail your favorite room.

*As you write your composition, remember to —*

☐ focus on a controlling idea that reflects a detailed description of your favorite room

☐ organize your ideas logically and link them with transitions

☐ include appropriate facts and details to illustrate your points

☐ make sure your composition is no longer than one page

# Progress Test 2

## Part 1: Basic Elements of Writing

**Questions 1–12: Read each sentence. Choose the best way to write the underlined part of the sentence. Fill in the circle of the correct answer on your answer document.**

**1** The elephant is <u>a amazing animal</u>.

  **A** a amazed animal
  **B** an amazing animal
  **C** the amazing animal
  **D** Make no change

**2** Most animals depend <u>in their environment</u> for food.

  **F** at their environment
  **G** through their environment
  **H** on their environment
  **J** Make no change

**3** <u>Baby deer needs</u> plenty of room to run around.

  **A** Baby deers needs
  **B** Baby deer need
  **C** Baby deers need
  **D** Make no change

**4** Crows and raccoons are capable of <u>making and using</u> simple tools.

  **F** made and used
  **G** make and use
  **H** makes and uses
  **J** Make no change

**5** <u>All mammals takes</u> care of their young, but most reptiles do not.

  **A** All mammals take
  **B** All mammals took
  **C** All mammal take
  **D** Make no change

**6** Some <u>intelligenter</u> animals, such as dolphins and chimpanzees, can learn to use words, signs, or sounds to communicate.

  **F** most intelligent
  **G** more intelligenter
  **H** more intelligent
  **J** Make no change

**7** One of these lizards <u>is</u> a gecko.

  **A** be
  **B** are
  **C** am
  **D** Make no change

**8** Wolves form family groups and care for <u>each one</u> throughout their lives.

  **F** each others
  **G** one another
  **H** others
  **J** Make no change

**GO ON**

**9** Chimpanzees are among the <u>smart</u> of all animals.

   **A** smarter

   **B** smartly

   **C** smartest

   **D** Make no change

**10** Sharks <u>have surviving</u> longer than most other species.

   **F** have survived

   **G** has survived

   **H** surviving

   **J** Make no change

**11** Some scientists predict that insects will take over the earth, <u>furthermore</u> others strongly disagree.

   **A** also

   **B** while

   **C** therefore

   **D** Make no change

**12** Both deer and elk <u>cross</u> this road.

   **F** crosses

   **G** crossing

   **H** to cross

   **J** Make no change

---

**Questions 13–18: Read each question and fill in the circle of the correct answer on your answer document.**

**13** How can this sentence best be expanded by adding interesting details?

> David ran for the bus.

   **A** David ran for the bus and hurried to get there.

   **B** David was late so David ran for the bus.

   **C** Hearing the roar of an engine, David dropped his spoon and ran for the bus.

   **D** David ran quickly for the bus that was big and yellow and outside his house.

**14** How can this sentence best be expanded to make it more interesting?

> Karis and her friends passed in their homework.

   **F** Karis and her two friends passed in their homework late.

   **G** Karis and her two friends proudly passed in their English homework on time.

   **H** Karis and her silly friends passed in their homework and then they laughed.

   **J** Karis and her friends and basically everyone else in the class passed in their homework on time—well, practically on time, just before the bell rang at least.

**15** Why should the following sentence be revised?

> The math book was handed to the teacher.

A  The subject and verb do not agree.

B  It is written in the active voice.

C  It is written in the passive voice.

D  The pronoun and noun do not agree.

**16** Which is the best way to combine these two sentences?

> Learning French is difficult.
>
> French is my favorite class.

F  Learning French is difficult, French is my favorite class.

G  Learning French is difficult, but French is still my favorite class.

H  Learning French and French class are difficult but my favorite.

J  Even though learning French is difficult, class is still my favorite.

**17** Which is the best way to combine these two sentences?

> Jeffrey did not come to practice today.
>
> Tyler did not come to practice either.

A  Jeffrey did not come to practice today, Tyler didn't either.

B  Jeffrey did not come and Tyler did not come to practice today.

C  To practice today, Jeffrey and Tyler did not come.

D  Neither Jeffrey nor Tyler came to practice today.

**18** Which is the best way to improve this sentence to make it more interesting?

> Maya likes art class and likes to paint.

F  Maya loves art class and can spend hours painting a picture.

G  My friend Maya is nice and she likes art class and likes to paint.

H  Maya likes art class, and she also really likes to paint.

J  Art class is what Maya likes, and she likes to paint pictures, too.

**GO ON**

Questions 19–20: A student wrote this paragraph. It may need some changes or corrections. Read the paragraph. Then read each question. Fill in the circle of the correct answer on your answer document.

## Cliff Dwellers

(1) The Anasazi lived in parts of Arizona and Colorado thousands of years ago. (2) Anthropologists study their cliff dwellings to try to find clues about how they lived. (3) These cliffs are difficult to climb, and the caves are hidden. (4) Anthropologists guess that the Anasazi made these cliff dwellings for protection and safety. (5) I know how hard climbing a cliff is. (6) I can't imagine climbing cliffs every day. (7) Despite their safe cliff dwellings, the Anasazi people mysteriously disappeared. (8) No one really knows what happened to them.

**19** What type of paragraph is this?

  **A** expository

  **B** persuasive

  **C** response to a text

  **D** narrative

**20** Which two sentences should be removed to improve this paragraph?

  **F** sentences 1 and 2

  **G** sentences 3 and 4

  **H** sentences 5 and 6

  **J** sentences 7 and 8

# Part 2: Proofreading and Editing

Questions 21–30: Read the passages. Choose the best way to write each underlined part. Fill in the circle of the correct answer on your answer document.

Last week we went to the movies. Anthony and I saw 'Bridge to
                                                        **21**

Terabithia.' That movie is <u>incredible</u>! It tells the story of a lonely young
                              **22**

<u>boy . . . Jesse . . . and</u> his friendship with the <u>girl whom lives</u> next door.
            **23**                                        **24**

The characters in the movie are wonderful, and the setting is really

beautiful. <u>*Bridge to . . .*</u> is now my favorite film!
            **25**

**21** A *Bridge to Terabithia*.
    B "Bridge to Terabithia".
    C Bridge to Terabithia.
    D Make no change

**22** F increddible
    G incredibul
    H inkredible
    J Make no change

**23** A boy: Jesse and
    B boy (Jesse) and
    C boy; Jesse; and
    D Make no change

**24** F girl who lives
    G girl whom lived
    H girl whose lives
    J Make no change

**25** A *Bridge to (. . .)* is
    B *Bridge to . . . .* is
    C *Bridge to [. . .]* is
    D Make no change

GO ON

December 7, 2011

Dear Jennifer:
**26**

   How are you? I <u>can't hardly wait</u> to come and visit you. Vacation
**27**

is less than a month away. I have so much to tell you <u>about school, my</u>
**28**

<u>friends, and my new puppy.</u> Write soon to tell me what kinds of clothes

to bring for my visit. I don't know <u>weather we</u> should plan to go skiing.
**29**

<u>Your best friend,</u>
**30**
Melanie

**26 F** Dear Jennifer,
   **G** Dear Jennifer.
   **H** Dear Jennifer!
   **J** Make no change

**27 A** cannot hardly wait
   **B** hardly can't wait
   **C** can hardly wait
   **D** Make no change

**28 F** about school, my friends; and my
     new puppy.
   **G** about school, my friends—and my
     new puppy.
   **H** about school my friends and my
     new puppy.
   **J** Make no change

**29 A** whether we
   **B** which we
   **C** however we
   **D** Make no change

**30 F** Your Best Friend,
   **G** Your Best friend,
   **H** your best friend,
   **J** Make no change

## Part 3: Writing                                              Expository

**READ**

Although some of us are better at making things than others, each of us knows how to make something. It might be a paper airplane, a bracelet, a toy or puppet, a kite, or something else.

**THINK**

Think of something different or interesting that you know how to make. What materials do you need? What are the specific steps required to make it?

**WRITE**

Write an expository essay explaining in detail how to make the thing you choose.

*As you write your composition, remember to —*

☐ focus on a controlling idea that reflects a detailed description of how to make your chosen object

☐ organize your ideas logically and link them with transitions

☐ include appropriate facts and details to illustrate your points

☐ make sure your composition is no longer than one page

# Post-test

## Part 1: Basic Elements of Writing

---

**Questions 1–12: Read each sentence. Choose the best way to write the underlined part of the sentence. Fill in the circle of the correct answer on your answer document.**

---

**1** Skateboarding and snowboarding are different, but <u>it has</u> many similarities.

  **A**  it had
  **B**  them has
  **C**  they have
  **D**  Make no change

**2** Both sports <u>are becoming</u> quite popular in the last decade.

  **F**  have become
  **G**  are become
  **H**  becoming
  **J**  Make no change

**3** In both sports, <u>participants uses</u> many of the same skills to ride and do tricks.

  **A**  participant uses
  **B**  participants use
  **C**  participants using
  **D**  Make no change

**4** Snowboarding <u>is easier</u> to learn than skateboarding.

  **F**  is easily
  **G**  is more easy
  **H**  is easiest
  **J**  Make no change

**5** Participants in both sports <u>wearing</u> helmets and gloves.

  **A**  worn
  **B**  wear
  **C**  weared
  **D**  Make no change

**6** In the halfpipe contest, snowboarders leap <u>highly</u> into the air.

  **F**  high
  **G**  highest
  **H**  more high
  **J**  Make no change

**7** I can list several differences <u>at the two</u> sports.

  **A**  of the two
  **B**  between the two
  **C**  to the two
  **D**  Make no change

**8** Skateboarders ride on <u>pavement on the other hand, snowboarders</u> ride on snow.

  **F**  pavement on the other hand snowboarders
  **G**  pavement. on the other hand, snowboarders
  **H**  pavement; on the other hand, snowboarders
  **J**  Make no change

**9** Some ski resorts try to attract snowboarders by making special trails <u>for them</u>.

   **A** for they
   **B** for it
   **C** for themselves
   **D** Make no change

**10** Snowboarding is the <u>greater</u> sport I have ever tried!

   **F** great
   **G** greatest
   **H** most great
   **J** Make no change

**11** Most of my friends <u>likes</u> to skateboard in the park.

   **A** like
   **B** liking
   **C** is liked
   **D** Make no change

**12** Jeremy rides down the railing <u>quick and smooth</u>.

   **F** quick and smoothly
   **G** quickly and smooth
   **H** quickly and smoothly
   **J** Make no change

---

**Questions 13–18: Read each question and fill in the circle of the correct answer on your answer document.**

**13** Which is a complete sentence written correctly?

   **A** Classical music, as my father likes.
   **B** The music of Mozart and Beethoven, for example.
   **C** For centuries, what is now known as classical music.
   **D** Why do people call this music "classical"?

**14** Which is a run-on sentence and should be written as two sentences?

   **F** On weekends I play drums in a rock group in school I play percussion in the band.
   **G** Rock music is fun, while classical music is challenging.
   **H** I enjoy listening to and playing both kinds of music.
   **J** Bach is my favorite classical composer, and Jonas Brothers is my favorite rock band.

**15** Which is the best way to combine these two sentences?

> Pachelbel wrote music for church services.
>
> Pachelbel also wrote music for weddings.

   **A** Pachelbel wrote music for church services and wrote music for weddings.
   **B** Pachelbel wrote music for church services and weddings.
   **C** Music for church services and also weddings was written by Pachelbel.
   **D** Music for church services, and Pachelbel also wrote music for weddings.

**GO ON**

**16** Which is the best way to combine these two sentences?

> Beethoven was deaf, but he composed music.
>
> John Stanley was blind, but he composed music.

**F** Beethoven was deaf and blind, but John Stanley composed music.

**G** Beethoven composed music, John Stanley was blind and composed music.

**H** Even though Beethoven was deaf and John Stanley was blind, they both composed music.

**J** Even though Beethoven was deaf and even though John Stanley was blind, Beethoven and John Stanley composed music.

**17** Which is an interrogative sentence that should end with a question mark?

**A** Beethoven is best known for his Ninth Symphony

**B** That is why I enjoy it so much

**C** I wonder if you have a favorite piece of classical music

**D** Are you familiar with Handel's *Messiah*

**18** Which is a declarative sentence that should end with a period?

**F** I wonder which piece we'll hear first

**G** Where did you learn to play the cello

**H** What a beautiful song

**J** Do you know the name of this piece

---

**Questions 19–20:** A student wrote this paragraph about volunteering. It may need changes or corrections. Read the paragraph. Then each question. Fill in the circle of the correct answer on your answer document.

### Helping Others

Yesterday I started my job as a volunteer at the hospital. I am working as a nurse's aide on the children's floor. I was very nervous when my dad dropped me off. I had never really spent much time in a hospital, but I knew I wanted to learn about what went on there. I also wanted to help sick kids. My first job was to bring all the kids their breakfasts. That was fun! Next week I look forward to playing with them in the rec room.

**19** What type of paragraph is this?

**A** expository

**B** persuasive

**C** response to a text

**D** narrative

**20** Which detail sentence could best be added just before the last sentence?

**F** I was having so much fun that the time passed quickly.

**G** The nurses were nice and helpful.

**H** I may stop by for a visit this week.

**J** I couldn't understand the job.

GO ON

# Part 2: Proofreading and Editing

Questions 21–30: Read the passages. Choose the best way to write each underlined part. Fill in the circle of the correct answer on your answer document.

Jacob Lawrence was an African American artist during the

second half of the <u>twenty century</u>. In his paintings, he often showed
**21**

the struggles faced by African Americans. For example, in the

*Migrant* series, he completed 60 paintings showing the migration

of African Americans from the South to the North. As my teacher

explained, "<u>[Lawrence]</u> painted simple characters in mostly
**22**

<u>plain colors</u>, but his paintings told of some important events in
**23**

American <u>histery</u>." You can learn more about this important artist if
**24**

you tune into the <u>nbc</u> program, "An Artist at Work."
**25**

**21 A** 20 century
   **B** twentyeth century
   **C** 20th century
   **D** Make no change

**22 F** '[Lawrence]
   **G** "[Lawrence (he)]
   **H** ["Lawrence"]
   **J** Make no change

**23 A** planed colors
   **B** plane colors
   **C** plainly colors
   **D** Make no change

**24 F** history
   **G** histerry
   **H** hisstory
   **J** Make no change

**25 A** N.B.C.
   **B** NBC
   **C** N.B.c
   **D** Make no change

Name _____ Date _____

March 5, 2011

Editor
*Model Trains Magazine*
5610 Park Street NW
<u>Washington, dc</u> 20036
   **26**
Dear Editor:

I am an avid reader of your magazine. <u>Especially love</u> the pictures and sample set-ups.
                                            **27**

I am writing to ask why <u>last months issue</u> had no set-up column or pictures. My friend
                          **28**

says you plan to discontinue the set-up column. He heard the news at a local meeting

sponsored by the organization <u>model trains of america</u>. When my friend gave me the
                                            **29**

news, I said, <u>"You've got to be kidding"!</u> I really hope this isn't true. Please keep the
              **30**

set-up column for model train lovers like me!

Sincerely,

Jacob Hiltman

**26 F** Washington, DC
   **G** Washington, d.c.
   **H** Washington, D.c.
   **J** Make no change

**27 A** Especially loving
   **B** Especially love me
   **C** I especially love
   **D** Make no change

**28 F** last months' issue
   **G** last month's issue
   **H** last months issues
   **J** Make no change

**29 A** model trains of America
   **B** Model trains of America
   **C** Model Trains of America
   **D** Make no change

**30 F** 'You've got to be kidding!'
   **G** You've got to be kidding!
   **H** "You've got to be kidding!"
   **J** Make no change

**Part 3: Writing**  **Narrative**

**READ**

During the course of a school year we have all kinds of experiences, both good and bad. Sometimes the disappointments stay in our minds, but mostly it's the enjoyable experiences that we remember.

**THINK**

Think of one experience you had during this school year that you really enjoyed. What happened? Who was present? Where did this experience take place?

**WRITE**

Write a narrative essay telling the story of your enjoyable experience.

*As you write your composition, remember to —*

☐ focus on a controlling idea that reflects the story of your most enjoyable experience this school year

☐ organize your ideas logically and link them with transitions

☐ include appropriate facts and details about the event and communicate its importance

☐ make sure your composition is no longer than one page